THE BUSINESS OF PARTYING:

Q&A Sessions with Nightlife Hospitality Professionals

ALANA UDWIN

The Business of Partying:
Q&A SESSIONS WITH NIGHTLIFE HOSPITALITY PROFESSIONALS

iUniverse books may be ordered through booksellers or by contacting:

iUniverse
1663 Liberty Drive
Bloomington, IN 47403
www.iuniverse.com
844-349-9409

Cover photograph: World Red Eye
Author photograph: Brianna DeJesus-Banos

ISBN: 978-1-6632-1564-2 (sc)
ISBN: 978-1-6632-1565-9 (e)

Library of Congress Control Number: 2020925806

Print information available on the last page.

iUniverse rev. date: 01/12/2021

To my Zimbabwean Grandpa Saul, whom I never had the chance to meet, but whom I thank every single day for his entrepreneurial spirit and fearlessness to go after what sets one's soul on fire. His memories and life lessons live on through the copious stories that my dad, family, and Saul's close friends proudly share. I hope to be half the business pioneer, parent, and influential leader that Saul Udwin was.

ACKNOWLEDGMENTS

Thank you to my family for their unconditional support, especially my mom and sister, who were the most patient editors and truly helped me express my visions through words. Also, thank you to my parents for always trusting me when I go out to nightlife venues. Yes, Dad, I know you went to Studio 54 once. And yes, Mom, I'll take you clubbing.

Thank you to my friends for being the best cheerleaders and keeping me motivated to finish this passion project.

Thank you to my professors and advisors who encouraged me to explore this topic that is rarely studied in an academic setting.

Finally, thank you to my inspiring interviewees for their willingness to share their expertise and wealth of knowledge. Thank you for answering my burning questions about the industry that I wanted to understand so badly.

I will be forever grateful for everyone's kindness and cooperation throughout this process.

CONTENTS

Introduction 1

Chapter 1 Marketing Nightlife Hospitality 5

Chapter 2 Las Vegas—Ryan Levine 13

Chapter 3 Los Angeles—Nick Montealegre and Frankie Delgado 21

Chapter 4 New York City—Daniel Olarte Reina 47

Chapter 5 Boston—Alyssa McCourt 65

Chapter 6 Chicago—Steve Harris 75

Chapter 7 Austin—Jack Zimmermann and Matthew Napolilli 85

Chapter 8 Atlanta—Michael Krohngold 109

Chapter 9 Miami—Jason Odio 115

Chapter 10 Main Takeaways 123

INTRODUCTION

I want to make this clear: I am not writing this book because I love to party. Well, I do, but it is more than that. Ever since I was a little girl, I have been intrigued by live entertainment, and that curiosity has grown stronger throughout my young adulthood. When playing with dolls or stuffed animals as a child, I always made them my audience members and put on shows for them. I even convinced my parents to host my eighth birthday party at a small nightclub in South Florida with an appearance from a Justin Timberlake look-alike. One can assume my sweet sixteen was also anything but boring. Located in a bowling alley turned "nightclub," it was one of the biggest dance parties of the year.

My yearning for live entertainment amplified during my time at Cornell University. Since my freshman year of college, I have been an executive board member of Slope Day, Cornell's annual end-of-the-year music festival with over sixteen thousand attendees. I am proud and excited to be the executive director when I am a senior, where I will lead the six-member board to orchestrate all aspects of the biggest event of the year. Running Slope Day is similar to operating a nightclub in the sense that there are musical performers to book and partygoers to please. Those partygoers just happen to be my fellow Cornell students. Through this dream role, I have learned firsthand how to design a memorable show and throw an epic party.

In the nightlife industry, nightclub owners essentially put on a show every single night. The industry as a whole incorporates everything from music to dance, talent, celebrities, fashion, and many other cultural aspects. The nightlife industry is all about creating moments. Across the globe, it is a part of every city's culture, tourism, and entertainment. Cultural trends are integral to this business because the nightlife experience needs to reflect the identity of the city and crowd and adapt as that identity evolves.

The adrenaline I get from experiencing nightlife productions is probably more than the average partygoer. Most partygoers simply show up, have a good time, and leave. When I go out to a nightclub, I naturally analyze all the details and moving pieces of the night. I feel electrified when the DJ gets behind the booth, the bass drops in the song, the lights sync to the beat of the music, the alcohol bottles are paraded out with glimmering sparklers, and the crowd goes wild. The industry has certainly shifted from the era of discotheques and pubs that emerged after Prohibition. In today's society, nightclubs offer different types of glamorous, profitable parties. The nightlife industry might seem like little more than partying, but it is one of the highest revenue-generating industries in major cities across the United States. It is an exciting and extremely tough sector of the service, hospitality, and entertainment industries.

My serious interest in nightlife sparked during my first job, which was at World Red Eye, a multimedia agency based in Miami that makes a fortune capturing nightlife moments. The company sends photographers out to the top Miami nightclubs every night to capture the party and then catalog the best moments on WorldRedEye.com. I was captivated by how the photographers were able to capture photos that told the stories of people's nights out. Nightclubs across the country also hire photographers and post the photos online, but I was impressed by World Red Eye's website platform and editorial creativity, selecting specific photos and curating the story of that particular night. Seth Browarnik, the founder of World Red Eye, meticulously trains his photographers to capture the venue and wide array of nightlife characters while still giving his team the freedom to maintain their creative perspective. World Red Eye truly helps nightclubs make the intangible tangible by illustrating the moments that make people want to experience those Miami venues themselves.

After World Red Eye, over the past couple of years, I have held numerous positions in the entertainment, nightlife, hospitality, and communications fields. I have been fortunate enough to work in an array of venues ranging from a local Boston nightclub to "The World's Most Famous Arena," Madison Square Garden in the Big Apple. After experiencing nightlife hospitality in large US cities, including Miami, Los Angeles, New York City, Boston, and Las Vegas—as well as globally in Europe, South Africa, and Australia—I became interested in what makes each individual nightlife venue a unique and lucrative experience. I found myself curious about what influenced people to go to one venue over another when most of them offer similar experiences. This is the challenge that all nightclub owners face and the reason why they have to get the combination of production, creativity, strategy, and operation in nightlife hospitality right.

I was ecstatic when Cornell University gave me the opportunity to conduct an independent study, in the form of a book, on any topic of my choice because this felt like the ideal avenue to explore my passion for the nightlife industry and distribute my findings with others who are interested. Progressing from my innate draw to nightlife, I am now fascinated by the industry from a partygoer perspective as well as from a business mindset. These late-night venues are places for people to let loose and live life, and I relish how nightlife can bring people so much joy and memories that can last a lifetime.

In this book, written during my junior and senior years at Cornell, I unveil what actually goes into creating a nightlife experience and the reasons different nightclubs are successful in their own ways. This interview-based book consists of in-depth discussions, through emails and phone calls, with venerable nightlife professionals in cities with prominent nightlife scenes, including Las Vegas, Los Angeles, New York City, Boston, Chicago, Austin, Atlanta, and Miami. I uncover how these experts entered the field, their nightlife business model, and what makes their venues thrive. These interviews also awarded me the opportunity to ask the deeper questions that always race through my mind when I am in clubs and that I have been eager to ask nightlife professionals for years.

There are thousands of nightlife venues I have yet to experience, but the experts I interviewed provide an ample amount of industry knowledge and have compelling stories worth sharing. After speaking with the interviewees, it was evident that they have not only the skills necessary to prosper in the nightlife industry but also the passion and personality to keep these nightclubs popular and profitable night after night. I am not here to compare these clubs' revenues but rather to understand the similarities and differences in their strategies. Every venue has its own atmosphere and method.

Whether I was doing research for my classes or this book, I noticed the lack of professionally written books about the nightlife business. Many guides to the industry were written years ago and did not seem relevant to today's nightlife culture. My research process for this book was comprised of gathering insights from my school papers, constantly browsing the internet, reading an abundance of articles, watching films and documentaries, listening to podcasts, visiting museum exhibits, analyzing social media, talking to anyone and everyone, and of course going to the clubs to see it for myself. Discovering new things and making connections to the industry even when I was not seeking to was one of the most gratifying parts of this process.

The nightlife pros in this book are essentially purveyors of partying. Some of them are veterans turned experts, and some are just making their mark on the industry. Regardless of their stature in the business, they are all making an impact on the current nightlife culture. I thoroughly enjoyed hearing each individual's story and approach to nightlife, and I hope you do too! This industry, like any other, is always changing, but many of the points these experts made will surely stand the test of time. Now, please come behind the velvet rope with me and learn how these talented nightlife mavens throw parties for a living.

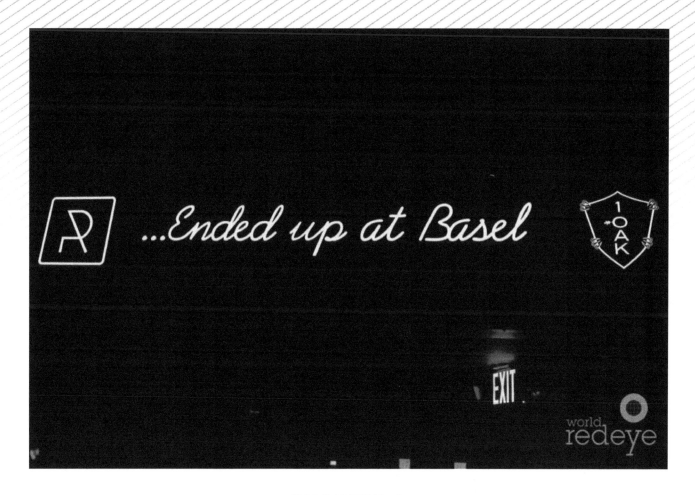

CHAPTER 1:
MARKETING NIGHTLIFE HOSPITALITY

Nightlife hospitality encompasses marketing an experience-based product. Each nightclub has its own vibe, so it takes creative marketing to successfully showcase what the nightlife experience will be like. Like any other industry, integrated marketing strategies to promote the nightlife brand through a variety of campaigns on every type of channel are imperative in order to achieve a recognizable, remunerative brand. Back in the day, word of mouth was basically the only way to build hype about a new nightclub or a fun party. Later, flyers were printed, and street teams handed out quarter cards and other promotional materials. Both of those methods are still used, but social media has taken today's nightlife marketing to a new level. Now there is not only word of mouth but also a vast amount of "word of eye." Partygoers are posting everything from the neon signs that are hanging in the club to countless selfies of them partying at hotspots. In this industry, the customers help tell the venue's story, so nightclub marketing managers certainly want to steer them in the right direction. Unlike other sectors of the service industry, clubbing is not an experience you can gather information about from a mere Yelp or Facebook review. This chapter dissects how and why diverse marketing strategies are used to promote a nightclub, and it provides a few examples of marketing tactics that I have found to be especially engaging. The nightlife marketing plan consists of typical marketing procedures with a heavier focus on a handful that are particularly effective for the nightlife industry. There are always exceptions as well. The marketing tactics range from traditional and basic to more current and customized, including but not limited to word of mouth and word of eye, public relations and social media, brand image and brand partnerships, promotional content and street promoters, and weekly programming and special events.

My concentration in hospitality marketing is primarily through the School of Hotel Administration at Cornell University, meaning my knowledge of marketing principles, consumer behavior, brand management, and media are taught from a hospitality industry perspective. That is how I initially deciphered the differences between marketing nightlife and other experiences and discerned how nightlife marketing affects the overall operation of nightclubs. Overall, a nightlife company's brand creativity, brand visibility, and brand consistency need to be properly executed by harmonizing traditional and current marketing tactics.

Word of Mouth and Word of Eye

The first two marketing tactics I am going to talk about are word of mouth and word of eye. Word of eye involves brand recognition through visual signifiers such as a logo, slogan, or image. This tactic is successful if people can name the nightlife brand or venue without being explicitly exposed to the club's name, but rather by seeing the visual attributes. It is a prominent form of word of mouth nowadays, thanks to the popularity of social media. Instead of telling people where they are going, partygoers now typically post where they are partying. Word of eye, especially on platforms like Instagram and Snapchat, is a cost-efficient marketing tactic because partygoers are essentially marketing the venue for free by posting on their accounts and reaching audiences that a club's marketing manager may not access.

I have been awfully impressed with how some nightlife marketers are able to subtly promote their brands and then encourage partygoers to market the clubs for them. As I mentioned earlier, a current nightlife trend is neon signs. Several nightlife venues have either a neon sign of lyrics, quotes, sayings, designs, or a cool art piece that is aesthetically pleasing to post. People then associate the venue with that art piece and know where someone is partying without them posting the actual name of the venue. For example, 1OAK, with venues in Los Angeles and New York City, is renowned for its "Started out at the Darby, ended up at 1OAK" line, quoting lyrics from Jay Z's song "Beach Is Better." Partygoers can expect to see neon signs with the line inside 1OAK. Another example in Los Angeles is Doheny Room's "Everything is going to be fucking amazing" neon sign, which sits on the wall above the staircase where partygoers enter and exit the club. The neon sign trend is also prevalent in other countries, such as the London Reign Showclub's neon angel wings to which partygoers flock to take endless photos as they enter the club. Partygoers do not even need to tag the venue on social media or write a caption mentioning where they are because the sign is a well-known indicator for people in the London nightlife scene. Moreover, many venues have branded electronic photo booths so when partygoers post their photo booth pictures, the venue's logo is automatically included for more free brand exposure. The more brand exposure, the better, but the subtle brand inclusions and image references are more favorable for maintaining a club's cool factor.

Another key opportunity to increase brand visibility is through the bottle parades. Nightclubs can take advantage of the bottle parades and utilize them for marketing purposes by having the bottle servers carry branded signs along with the bottles and sparklers to the VIP tables. The bottle parades are a main attraction, so if partygoers are going to post anything from their night on social media, it will probably be that. Therefore, nightclub marketers ensure that the brand name is included in all the photos and videos. The clubs do not want to advertise their brand to the point of begging people to party there. They want to encourage partygoers to show they are partying there, so more people will want to also.

Word of eye is not replacing word of mouth by any means, but it is complementing it. Word of mouth in nightlife goes beyond people just mentioning the venue in conversation or suggesting it for a night out among a group of friends. First, famous artists and rappers frequently name-drop nightclub brands, such as Kanye West and Lil Wayne mentioning LIV Miami in their songs, G-Eazy shouting out E11EVEN Miami, or Drake rapping about Greystone, a former Los Angeles club. Second, word of mouth plays a big role in the speakeasy category of nightlife. It is a part of their cool factor in addition to their Prohibition vibe. Speakeasies are a huge part of Sydney, Australia's nightlife scene. When I was studying abroad there, we would do speakeasy crawls, which were like fun scavenger hunts because each one was sneakily located, and there was no signage whatsoever. In contrast to nightclubs, speakeasies aim to remain discreet and are not promoted a ton, so word of mouth is especially important for them to get customers through their doors.

World Red Eye, the multimedia agency I mentioned earlier, has full potential to contribute to nightclubs' word of eye. The company is able to make the intangible tangible by capturing the venue, partygoers, DJs, celebrities, bottle service, dancers, and other entertainment and then posting the photos online and on social media. People who are featured in the photos then have the opportunity to post them on their own social media accounts, further expanding the club's reach. People who were not at the club that night but see the posted photos may be inspired to experience that party in the future. Similar to "a picture is worth a thousand words," a nightclub's photo can truly encapsulate the entire experience.

Public Relations and Social Media

A critical part of traditional marketing that is here to stay is public relations. Public relations (PR) has always been a powerful marketing tactic because every venue wants to be featured in magazines, in newspapers, and online to increase brand visibility in the media. This is why celebrity appearances are heavily used as a marketing ploy as well. Celebrity appearances can range from Rick Ross showing up to sing two or three of his big hits to Kim Kardashian celebrating her birthday at the venue. Celebrity appearances are efficacious for nightlife PR because a celebrity appearance is almost a guaranteed press feature for the club. Celebrities are a driving force in solidifying a club's social status and influencing people to choose one venue over another. Hosting a celebrity's birthday celebration or other occasion at the club is a great excuse to get celebrities in the door and photographed partying there. In Las Vegas, megaclubs are known for their extensive list of DJ residencies each year, and the announcement of the residency lineup is always a solid press opportunity for both the clubs and the DJs who earned the deal.

Regarding social media, I have seen nightlife venues use the platforms in various ways. Each nightlife brand has a distinct vibe, and its social media accounts should align with it. My interviewees explain this further, but social media is a great way to show what the vibe will be, what the crowd is like, who is performing, what music will be played, the brands of alcohol they serve, and more. Some venues like to post graphically designed flyers that include information about their upcoming parties, including which DJ is performing, ticket prices, how to make VIP table reservations, and whether there is a special theme that night. Other venues take the Pinterest board approach and post on-brand photos that do not necessarily show the venue but convey the general vibe of the place on their page. For instance, The Bungalow in Los Angeles posts an array of beachy California pictures to portray the beachy vibe that the physical venue embodies. This technique makes the brand more eye-catching and interesting to see when scrolling through your Instagram feed. The goal is to catch people's attention with cool, on-brand content that will effectively remind them to go to the venue that night.

Branding

I personally admire nightclubs that use wordplay to manipulate the brand's name into catchy slogans, sayings, hashtags, and more. Brand creativity is a bonus for a nightlife brand because it helps the brand name stick; the brand is more fun to say, see, and interact with. For instance, 1OAK stands for "One of a Kind," so the club promotes every party and partygoer as being one of a kind. Another prime example is E11EVEN Miami's play with the number eleven. "Being a ten" makes you perfect or very attractive, so the club promotes every party and partygoer as better than perfect, or "elevens." A third example is London Reign Showclub alluding to London's rainy weather with partygoers "making it reign" with dollar bills in the club. The clever play on words or sayings helps immensely with brand visibility and brand consistency because they are typically incorporated into social media hashtags, merchandise, and other marketing areas.

Moreover, brand partnerships are important because they help clubs in a variety of ways, including cutting costs, increasing brand awareness, enhancing their brand image, and breaking up a venue's weekly programming by making some nights extra special or occasion specific. One of the main types of brand partnership involves nightlife groups arranging pop-up clubs in different cities, such as TAO Group partnering with Ultra Music Festival in Miami to host the VIP tent, or 1OAK teaming up with Rockwell Miami during Art Basel Miami. These brand collaborations are mutually beneficial for the nightlife and entertainment companies because they add credibility to both brands and expand their clienteles. For example, the Rockwell partygoers in Miami will be more inclined to go to 1OAK when they visit New York City or Los Angeles, and vice versa. These co-branded experiences are essentially experiential marketing because they are a tease of what it is like to party at both clubs.

Digital and Street Promotion

I am a huge fan of promotional videos as a marketing tool for nightlife because partygoers can catch a glimpse of the club in action instead of just a static photo. The engaging videos truly help nightlife consumers visualize the club experience that cannot always be described in words. The marketers know exactly what to include in the promotional videos: shots of the DJ, dancers, attractive partygoers, booze, bottle parades with sparklers and confetti, and more. XS at the Wynn and Encore Beach Club at Encore Las Vegas are particularly adept at promotional videos. Their videos have the music seamlessly synced up to the partygoers dancing, fire and lights going off, and DJs performing. They also choose the best songs and remixes to play in the videos. Furthermore, XS and Encore are renowned for their top-tier DJ residencies, and the promotional videos that are released every few months for their upcoming residency lineups are innovative and unparalleled. Props to them.

In cities like Las Vegas and Miami, clubs will use outdoor marketing, including big billboards, to promote their venues and upcoming performers. Not all nightlife brands can afford outdoor marketing, but another nondigital marketing tactic that is imperative in the nightlife industry is street promotion. Most, if not all, venues hire promoters to seek out partygoers, especially females, to bring to the club and show them a positive experience of partying there. Promoters are part of word of mouth marketing, but social media has made their job a lot easier. Promoters simply post one photo about the club, and people will start messaging them to join the party. You will later read in my interviews about the pros and cons of modern-day, digitally infused street promoting. Sometimes people are hesitant about going out or indecisive about where they should go, so promoters are there to encourage and guide partygoers. I asked most of my interviewees about promoters' roles in their individual companies, and I even got to interview a professional promoting group that works for some of the top nightclubs in New York City.

Programming

Although special events are pivotal, so is normal weekly programming. Weekly programming includes the nights where this is the normal music, drinks, and entertainment but no special performer or occasion. Venues typically name their weekly nights, such as the famous LIV on Sunday at LIV Miami, and differentiate the nights with diverse music genres or themes. People then make certain parties part of their routine because they know which night they want to attend. Some nights like LIV on Sunday and Favela Beach at WALL Miami stick and become iconic, but once certain parties become dull, clubs can rebrand the night with a completely new name and vibe. This is necessary because music and cultural trends are always changing, so it is crucial that the programming remains current. Nightlife brands have definitely gotten more creative than just hosting "ladies' nights."

Nightlife venues also leverage holidays and special events like Art Basel, Fashion Week, Miami Music Week, concert after-parties, celebrity birthdays, and the Super Bowl to switch up their programming. These special events are often called layered events because the added layer of a holiday theme, celebration, or special performer makes the night a little more special, gives marketers and promoters a more distinct event to promote, and ultimately attracts larger crowds.

In conclusion, these are only a handful of nightlife marketing tactics, ideas, and examples. No matter what the nightlife brand represents, it is imperative that nightlife marketers stay consistent with that image and build popularity from it in order for the club to stand out in the cluttered nightlife market. With strong brand creativity, visibility, and consistency, nightclubs are likely to gain success and ensure longevity.

CHAPTER 2:
LAS VEGAS—RYAN LEVINE

"Every week is a new experience with new people from all over the world.
Such a true form of hospitality."

Ryan Levine graduated from Cornell University's School of Hotel Administration in 2017 and is currently the director of marketing for events and nightlife at MGM Resorts in Las Vegas. Ryan recently helped open the Mayfair Supper Club, a glamorous restaurant with dazzling supper club–style entertainment, at the Bellagio Resort and Casino. When this interview was conducted, he was the marketing director at Encore Beach Club in Wynn Las Vegas, which is one of the top-grossing nightclubs in Sin City. In between his roles at Wynn and MGM, Ryan was the director of nightlife marketing at the Palms Casino Resort in Vegas. Ryan's success in the nightlife industry comes as no surprise because he has passionately pursued a career in nightlife since his freshman year of college.

Las Vegas is renowned for being one of the largest hubs of nightlife venues in the United States. The famous Las Vegas Strip is full of some of the most prominent and highest revenue-generating hotels, casinos, and nightclubs in the world. The city is undoubtedly a party destination for everyone, and the nightlife scene consists of about eighty percent tourists and twenty percent locals.

When I met Ryan at Cornell a few years ago, I could automatically tell he was well-connected and knowledgeable about this industry. In 2014, he started the Nightlife Hospitality Club at Cornell, where he aimed to cultivate a better understanding of the industry and its relevance as an important revenue stream for hospitality companies. Through the Cornell club, he hosted industry professionals from around the country to speak and also arranged nightlife venue tours for members of the organization.

Ryan is a perfect example of the saying "You're never too young to chase your dream job." This interview with Ryan includes how his early initiative to learn about the industry, his internship experiences in college, his strong networking skills, and his personal drive put him ahead of the game when he officially entered the industry after college graduation. He took his deep interest for the industry in his freshman year of college and ran with it. I am proud to know him, and his success boldly represents what a Cornell University education paired with individual ambition can produce.

As a highly experienced hospitality and nightlife professional, Ryan has helped establish and operate an impressive array of notable venues in Las Vegas. Although this interview is specific to Ryan's experience at Wynn Las Vegas, it is evident that he applies the same knowledge and enthusiasm to every role he has in the nightlife industry. His future is bright, and I am eager to continue watching this fellow Cornellian shine.

Please enjoy learning more through my conversation with Ryan.

How did you get started in the nightlife industry?

I first became interested in the nightlife industry my freshman year at Cornell. Between my freshman and sophomore years, I interned at 1OAK NYC, getting the internship by reaching out to Scott Sartiano, the co-owner, with my interest. That summer, I learned a lot about an industry I wasn't too familiar with: marketing, operations, dynamics, etc. The next couple of summers, I would intern at Catch NYC, Gerber Group, and then at Wynn Las Vegas.

What made you want to work in nightlife?

My freshman year, I identified three things: (1) The nightlife industry was becoming increasingly integrated as an industry in hospitality. Since it was becoming successful, more money passed through it, which as a result allows the industry to be more regulated and less sketchy. (2) It is the best form of hospitality; one remembers one's experience (or doesn't) at a nightclub compared to a typical hotel room stay. (3) Nightclubs were becoming the destination for Las Vegas, which is a great indicator for future hospitality industry trends.

Describe your day-to-day and night-to-night responsibilities as nightlife marketing manager at Wynn.

Emails, strategy, meetings. I would say the majority of my day is meetings, consisting of communicating with the operations team of the club, communicating strategy with our digital marketing team at the resort, communicating with team on new initiatives either on venue or resort level, and finally the weekly Tuesday marketing meeting, where I have to have all my work together to present in front of the VP. Emails consist of back and forth with our design team on assets that need to be created, decor companies for future special events and their vision and cost, and other communications internally. The strategy is created in meetings or alone and implemented in email. I go into the venue on the busy days to make sure the photographer is getting the correct alcohol-sponsor photos; if there are special events, the decor needs to be coordinated, and to show face to network, since a lot of locals come in and out of the clubs. Locals are important to please since word of mouth marketing is the best form in Vegas.

What previous professional experiences have helped you most in this role?

Every internship, which I had nine in total since high school, and also the intuition gained from the overall hospitality and business classes taken from Cornell. I would say my internship at Wynn before getting a full-time offer helped me a lot with company norms and also learning the Vegas market.

What are some job perks that you enjoy?

Access to the best clubs in the world allows for amazing networking because it attracts people with great connections.

What makes Wynn different from a typical nightclub?

The customer experience. Any nightclub in Vegas can have the best talent, but the main differentiator is the experience and customer service. Second, the Wynn nightclubs are beautiful, boasting indoor and outdoor elements to all of them. Third, and something that contradicts the first point, we have the best DJ residents, but that's based on unique programming. We span all genres in EDM (electronic dance music), from deep house to heavy bass to mainstream.

What is different about Vegas nightlife culture versus other party destinations, such as Miami, Los Angeles, and New York City?

I love this question because it means you know the industry, meaning each city is one thousand percent different from each other.

(1) New York City: This is the city you build a nightlife brand, as a lot of the successful brands started here. Low barriers to entry, culture capital. Demographic wise, a mixture of local and transient.

(2) LA: majority local.

(3) Miami. I am least adept at Miami nightlife, but I know it's similar to New York. However, high barriers to entry because MMG and E11EVEN are major players.

(4) Vegas: Mostly transient, but locals are really important. High barriers to entry, as the clubs cost more than one hundred million dollars to build.

Describe the general components of a nightlife marketing plan. What goes into promoting the nightclub experience, and how does Wynn constantly build buzz and evolve to stay relevant?

A lot. The simplest breakdown is this:

(1) On property. Huge LED on the strip, in-room TVs, on-property signs, etc.

(2) Off property. Digital billboards, gym advertisements (huge place to capture locals), airport ads, LA static billboards, etc.

(3) Promoter team. The team that brings the crowd in to fill the club.

(4) Host team. The team that brings the bottle service customers into the club.

(5) Social media. Instagram feed strategy, Instagram story strategy to accompany the feed. Facebook, Twitter. What does the graphic look like? Is it a video or static image? Why release it on a certain day?

(6) Digital marketing. Money allocated to target individual demographics. An entire strategy based on specific situation and events to be marketed. Local event target locals, etc.

(7) Staff support. Are the two hundred plus staff members per venue pushing the current marketing on their socials, and in turn do their networks see the upcoming events?

(8) In-venue LED signage. Are we capturing the alcohol sponsor, which pays for a portion of expenses to be documented in the venue? Is decor needed for the event, like Halloween decor on Halloween? Does operations know of specific marketing initiatives? Etc.

Have there been measurable benefits from using social media? If so, what are they, and how have you measured them?

The main metric is ticket sales based on the use of social media. Ticket sales is a strong indicator of the revenue and also bottom-line performance for that day. If the ticket sales are high, that leads to a lot of people in venue, which equals high ticket sales revenue, high bar revenue, and table customers willing to spend more than their typical minimum, which leads to profit.

Who are some of your mentors, and why are they quality leaders in your eyes?

Sean Christie: One of the main founders of modern-day nightlife in Vegas. While he was at the Wynn, we connected, and he was one who allowed me my internship and allowed me to be at my full potential, even though I was an intern. He is a great teacher, and even though he was at that time COO, he took time to teach. He is now at MGM, but we still reconnect now and then. Great person.

Ronn Nicolli: Senior director of marketing, Wynn Nightlife. He is the most brilliant person I know, on another planet of intuition and knowledge for Las Vegas marketing. He empowers people, which is hard to find. By far the most creative person, if I haven't stressed that enough. Through working and observing, I have learned a million times more than I could ever learn in school.

How have recent events regarding Steve Wynn affected your job status or career outlook?

The company has changed immensely in leadership and the way the company is run currently.

How has working in the nightlife industry affected your own social life (sacrifices, trade-offs, access, etc.)?

This industry is definitely a lifestyle, six to seven days a week living it. Office, working in a club, hosting people who visit Vegas in the club—it is all-encompassing, and therefore you have to accept it. It's not for everyone. Vegas is such a unique city, probably one of a kind in the fact that there is a new batch of people coming in and out every week. Therefore, every week is a new experience with new people from all over the world. Such a true form of hospitality.

For the next generation of twenty-one-year-olds, how would you show them the ropes to the nightlife industry?

Intern in NYC first, because it's legal to eighteen and over. When you turn twenty-one, intern in Vegas.

(1) Join the NLHC at Cornell, and always keep the connection between nightlife industry leaders and the highest form of hospitality education present.

(2) Take beverage classes because it is the main revenue source of a nightclub.

(3) Listen to new music every day through podcasts. There is always new music to be exposed to. Keep going to music festivals for that too.

(4) Keep up-to-date with the news. Since nightlife has grown so big, it's not hard to find out what is happening.

Nick Montealegre

CHAPTER 3:
LOS ANGELES—NICK MONTEALEGRE AND FRANKIE DELGADO

"You're only as good as your last party."

Los Angeles nightlife is all about glamour, exclusivity, and celebrity orientation. I am thrilled that I got to speak to not only one but two of LA's nightlife doyens who were integral in making the scene what it is today and who are now running several of the hottest venues in the City of Angels. Nick Montealegre is the director of nightlife at SBE and oversees Doheny Room, Nightingale, and Hyde Sunset. Frankie Delgado gained his fame as a cast member on *The Hills* and *The Hills: New Beginnings,* and he runs some of the hottest parties at several of SBE's venues in LA, including Hyde Sunset. Nick and Frankie are both prominent names and faces in the nightlife industry and have proven that anything is possible with hard work, passion, and timing. Nick and Frankie both made the most of where they were partying, when they were partying, and with whom they were partying.

Frankie's business approach seems relatively consistent in his decisions to focus on the exclusivity factor, naturally leveraging his personal high-profile relationships while also making sure everyone, no matter who they are, feels and contributes to the energy at every party. Frankie is public-relations centric and focuses on getting celebrity coverage at these LA hotspots. If those places are good enough for celebrities, then partygoers will think it is good enough for them.

Throughout Nick's career, he has been unbelievable at pivoting and adapting to what is current. Nick focuses on curating the perfect music, vibe, and crowd. Nick stands out as one of the most forward-thinking experts I have ever spoken to, and his business acumen is the reason he is a chief leader in SBE's nightlife sector. He could run a nightclub with his eyes closed, and it would still succeed. He is on top of his game and already planning for the future by getting ahead of technology's continual disruption of every industry.

When speaking with Nick, I made very little edits because our conversation really painted the picture of his nightlife journey and thought processes behind his day-to-day management decisions. Nick continuously adapted to the times and environments he was in during his start in LA in the early 2000s. He is another expert where clubbing was his side hustle turned career due to the passion and proficiency he developed. It seems his enthusiasm for nightlife remains unwavering because I could feel his excitement through the phone when talking about celebrities and nightclubs. Nick has been part of many diverse nightlife venues, and he always had the natural ability to draw in large and vivacious crowds. Therefore when it came to managing his own venues, he knew exactly what he wanted and needed to do.

Something that Nick and Frankie both feel passionately about is training the next generation of nightlife employees and leadership. They contribute to the future of the nightlife industry in LA by putting time and energy into promoters, club operators, and other employees involved. Another piece of insight I gleamed from our conversations was their desire to set an example for partygoers regarding how to make their venues a safe space for big name celebrities. You will also recognize that Nick and Frankie emphasize how LA is more heavily driven by exclusivity, celebrities, and promoters than other cities mentioned in my book. Nick and Frankie have worked together for years and have influenced what the nightlife scene in LA currently looks like today.

Please enjoy learning more through my conversation with Nick.

How did you get started in the nightlife industry? What made you want to work in nightlife?

I was born in Costa Rica, but I grew up in LA. My parents divorced, and my dad took custody and raised me in Beverly Hills in a little apartment. We weren't wealthy or anything, but he wanted to make sure that I was in a good school district and grew up with some consistency because he didn't have that growing up. The reason I'm starting there is because in this industry, a lot of it is about your network and the people. Growing up in an affluent part of town and with kids who ended up becoming rich and famous definitely gave me a head start among people who were just trying to break into the industry. Everyone around me is the reason why I'm successful and why I got to where I am.

I graduated from Beverly Hills High School, but I didn't really know what I wanted to do, so I went to Santa Monica College for three years and was just getting by. I was always just a B student. Then, I transferred to UC Santa Barbara and finished up my last two years of school there. I did five years of college. In Santa Barbara, I studied political science mainly because I thought that was a way to get accepted, because my mom and stepdad both worked for the US embassy. They were living in Moscow at the time, and I would always visit them. For five summers in a row, I went to Moscow and spent three months out of the year working at the US embassy, and I partied out there and traveled. When I was writing my letter to the different schools, I was like, "Well, since I already worked at the embassy, I'm really into politics." I actually did like it at the time. It was right around 9/11, so it was interesting. I ended up getting straight As and graduating with honors. I really buckled down those last two years.

When I graduated, I really didn't know what I was going to do. I was going through a breakup, and I stayed in Santa Barbara. I was working at a used car dealership—a Volvo dealership—taking people on test drives. Then, I came back down to LA.

I had always been passionate about music, so I started a record label with my buddy, Leeron. His family was from Beverly Hills, and he was a wealthy kid, so he had the resources to fund it. It was called Block Ready Records. It was right around the time when Napster and LimeWire were big, so people weren't really paying for music much. We signed this rapper Big Steal, who was on the radio, and we also did a music video. It ended up completely flopping, and we didn't make any money really.

From then on, I lived in Leeron's parents' backhouse in Beverly Hills and worked for his father's diamond company. They sold raw diamonds downtown, so I was traveling to Orange County with diamonds. I didn't know what I was doing. I was just making money, getting by, but I was also going out.

I was back in LA from Santa Barbara, so I had my friends and was going to the clubs. Back then, there weren't that many promoters, and there weren't that many clubs. There was only one club you could go to on every night, and if you didn't get into that club, then you were shit out of luck. You could go to a bar or something, but there was only one club on each night that was the "it" spot. Bolthouse Productions and the Alliance were pretty much the only players in the club game.

I went to Friday night at Spider, which was supposed to be the popping spot. It was basically where Avalon is now. Spider just wasn't that fun, so there was nothing really fun to do on a Friday night. My friends and I were like, "Dude. We could throw a better party than this."

We randomly got a meeting with this guy, Med, who was about to be programming the remodel of the Roosevelt Hotel. It was me, Brick Williams, and Trevor Wright, who are my childhood friends. Trevor's now an actor, and Brick's in real estate. Back then, we all sat down with Med, and then he introduced us to this woman who was the boss lady at the Roosevelt, Amanda Demme. She was Ted Demme's widow. Ted Demme wrote and produced *Blow* and a bunch of other movies. She was a badass lady who was tough as nails and cool as fuck. She was our first in to the nightlife world. We pitched to her and said, "Listen. Let us help you throw a party on a Friday night. We can kill it." We sold her on everything, sold her the dream. She was like, "Okay. Fine. We'll give these kids a shot."

Then Friday comes around, and we invited everybody and their cousin and their cousins. We invited everyone. We didn't care. We had no filter. We gave her this long-ass guest list, and she basically tossed it in the garbage. She ran her door at the Roosevelt pool, the Tropicana by the pool. She was the toughest door in the world. The entire parking lot of the Roosevelt was filled with bodies, and nobody could get into this party. She herself had a crazy network. I'm talking really cool, Old Hollywood people like Al Pacino, Sharon Stone, and Marilyn Manson. It was a really wild, star-studded night.

We happened to have this girl Caroline D'Amore's birthday party, and Caroline was best friends with all the "it" girls at that time. Paris Hilton and Lindsay Lohan came out. Amanda thought we were amazing because we brought out the young celebrities and girls. She filtered our crowd and brought in the best people she thought were cool. The Friday night at the Roosevelt became the hottest party, the talk of the town. We had noise issues with the neighbor, but the music wasn't even that loud. It also wasn't even that great of a dynamic. It was just around the pool, and there weren't moving lights or anything. It was all about the crowd.

That kind of jump-started my nightlife career. Trevor had to leave to film a movie, so our promotional team became Nick & Brick Productions. We ended up opening Teddy's Lounge with Amanda, and that was also super exclusive. Prince would randomly pop up and do a performance. There would suddenly be a Britney Spears and Justin Timberlake dance-off. It was the kind of stuff that you hear about in the legends. Back then there were no camera phones, so nobody documented this stuff, which I think made famous people more inclined to go out.

After a while, we wanted to branch out. There was another club opening called Privilege that was owned by SBE. They approached us to see if we wanted to help out, and we did. Amanda didn't like that we were doing other nights and thought we were exclusive to her, so we ended up leaving the Roosevelt because it was time to leave anyway. We had already been there for a couple of years. We went with SBE and did Privilege and Lobby, which is where Doheny Room is now. Then we started doing Les Deux.

Les Deux was a huge success. We did the Wednesday night there with Tommy Alastra and Dean May, and we were packing it. *The Hills* filmed a bunch of episodes there, and it gained a ton of popularity. Then we did a party called Electric Fridays at Crimson. We were playing that electro music of the time in 2006–2007—Daft Punk, Mstrkrf, Justice. DJ AM and Steve Aoki had a party called Banana Split, which was more raw and underground, and we emulated it but introduced that sound to the mainstream and bottle service crowd. AM and Aoki blessed our party by spinning the first two nights consecutively for a fraction of their usual rate. It was a cool moment for us. Because of the Electric Fridays party, Dave Koral, a friend who grew up in Malibu, approached me and was like, "Listen, I want to open up my own spot, and I want you to partner with me." He was a local star QB who had tried to play football in the NFL, but he got injured. He still holds a ton of high school California records. At the time, Brick and I were having our differences, and I felt I was doing most of the work. He was going through some personal issues as well and didn't seem to care as much, so I basically stopped promoting with Brick, and we went our separate ways. I took more than a year off from working the clubs and started running poker games to make money.

Dave introduces me to our new business partner, Matt Bendik, who would handle operations for the new spot. Dave would finance the project, and I was the marketing and front of house. The three of us were under thirty. I was the oldest at twenty-nine. We decided on this location at 7969 Santa Monica Blvd and called it Voyeur. The space was great because the club had a topless license that was grandfathered in since before the city of West Hollywood was even a city. It was the Big Pussycat, where Frank Sinatra and the Rat Pack used to go to. To this day, it's one of the only places in California where you can legally have exposed nipple and liquor in the same room. The only stipulation was that the nipple had to be ten feet away from the liquor. We were like, "Okay. What do we do with this? We've got to utilize this somehow." We ended up building a trapeze net above everyone's heads. The dancers and performers could crawl around topless high up on the net. It was a cool, avant-garde, dark, very "eyes wide shut" experience. We obviously made it that there were no photos allowed because of all the toplessness and celebrities in attendance. Voyeur ended up being a major success. I had basically jumped from being a promoter to being a part owner, and I was programming all the DJs, handling the promotions, and doing what I do now, but just for this one venue. We brought on the Alliance guys, Josh Richman, Hartwell, and Frankie Delgado, who promoted Thursdays and Saturdays at Voyeur for three years. They were a major part of Voyeur's success as well. After three years, we had a falling out with the landlord partners, who were involved in the business as well. The mutual accountant was driving a Ferrari and a Lamborghini, and we ultimately found out that he was embezzling from the business.

Anyways, the venue closed, and around that time SBE, who is owned by Sam Nazarian, who went to the same high school as me and my sister, had a new club opening. I had worked with them as a promoter, and Costas, who was the VP there at the time, approached me to see if I was interested in coming on board and helping to open their latest venue. Voyeur had been kicking ass, and they had taken note since a couple venues had opened and closed against us. I felt like they thought, "Shit. If you can't beat them, acquire them." They lured me over and offered me a really good deal to come on board. It worked out perfect with the timing, and in 2010 we opened Greystone Manor with SBE. The Alliance were free agents as well, and we all came like a package deal. They did Thursdays and Saturdays at Greystone just like they did at Voyeur. We had other parties on different days that I was also in control of, but those nights were the backbone along with Made Sundays. Greystone was actually a record-breaking venue. It made nineteen million dollars the first year, which is unheard of. A ton of rappers mentioned Greystone in their rhymes—like, Drake shouted it out, "Greystone, twenty bottles that's on me." The Game also has a whole song actually called "Greystone." The Greystone Sunday party is somewhat of an institution and is still called that now even though the venue is now Nightingale ten years later.

As time went by, I helped SBE open other venues, and slowly but surely, I took on more and more responsibility as my position with the company grew and elevated. Also, we downsized the nightlife department, so now we're a pretty small unit. I currently oversee three venues in LA: Nightingale, Doheny Room, and Hyde Sunset. Nightingale is our big room venue where Greystone was, and we brought nightlife veteran Deborah Maguire to really drive that business, as well as the MADE team to continue their legendary Greystone Sunday Party. Doheny Room is near and dear to my heart because I grew up on Doheny right down the street. All my friends lived on Doheny, so that was kind of the name our crew repped—Doheny. It's super eclectic and tastefully done. Then we have Hyde Sunset, which is really our cornerstone, branding-wise. Frankie Delgado has been a real backbone to the venue and holds it down.

How is the nightlife scene in Los Angeles affected by the money versus exclusivity factor?

Exclusivity and an attention to the crowd quality is always something that creates longevity. I think the problem for stand-alone clubs, meaning they're not in a hotel and have to pay the rent, is that the number one focus ultimately becomes the clients. Because there are so many options with competition and real spenders are scarce, more and more you have to cater to the financial element. It's also not as judgmental of a scene anymore as LA used to be. Yes, if you go out, nine times out of ten you will find someone whom you recognize or who's considered famous, but real fame doesn't party like they used to in other decades because everyone has a surveillance device in their hands. I sometimes forget that people are even famous because they're just our friends. There used to be VIP rooms and almost segregated areas, but that doesn't work anymore because the truth is everyone knows when they're on the wrong side of the VIP. It's not a good feeling. Yeah, it might be cool for the few people who are in, but from a business standpoint, it's much healthier to make everyone who's in the entire club feel like a VIP and spread the energy. At other clubs in LA, they may have a specific area by the DJ where no one can get through, and it separates the haves and have-nots. All the promoters are in there. In my opinion, it's such a waste to have all the promoters in one area. What I do is put one promoter on this side of the room to hold down the energy over there, and I put someone else on the other side. You fill the corners so that everywhere you go, there is some energy, girls, and activity. Then it's not like, "Oh, that area sucks."

Seating the room is also an important aspect. It's like solving a puzzle. You make sure, "Okay. This is a bachelor party with twenty guys. We should definitely not put them at the first table when you walk in. You don't want to see twenty guys right there when you walk in. Let's put them over here, and let's put a promoter who has a girl's birthday party with a bunch of girls right next to them, so that they could maybe be introduced and start buying the girls drinks." It's like throwing an event every single night. It's crazy, the amount of money that we're making night in, night out and week in, week out. It's a really good business, to be honest.

How do you and your team foster relationships with your clients and partygoers and make sure that they choose your venues over others?

Well, first and foremost, I think service is a major part of the business. Service is about SOPs, which are standard operating procedures, and making sure that training is done well and that your staff is on point. That's just good management—making sure that the tables are bussed and staffed properly, so people aren't waiting for drinks, and there's a girl making shots for them at the table if they want them. That's key because people notice that stuff. I think without that quality service, people would still come if the party is good, but they wouldn't spend as much, and they wouldn't feel like their money is actually being spent well. At the end of the day, "You're only as good as your last party" is a phrase that's commonly used. What it means is that you have to maintain, be consistent, and always curate the best experience night after night in order to retain your clients and reputation. If not, there are other operators or promoters right out the door, right down the street, that are just waiting for the business and have a similar party with similar offerings. It is important to offer good service and ultimately offer a great experience. If people leave happy, they'll come back. Our teams have great relationships and foster them well.

Regarding your clubs' programming, how do you decide which nights you want to be just a normal night with a DJ versus the nights with special performances or celebrity appearances?

We'll have special performances at Hyde or Nightingale sometimes. Typically, Doheny Room not as much just because it's a smaller venue. It comes down to making sure you see an ROI (return on investment). If you spend fifteen thousand dollars for Wiz Khalifa or something, then you've got to make sure that you're making at least fifteen thousand dollars or more than you normally would that night. Deciding which nights to have special performances kind of depends on the landscape of what else is happening. Sometimes if it's a major weekend like Memorial Day weekend or another three-day weekend, we'll have major talent on Sunday, knowing that people will probably spend more money than they would on a normal Sunday because they won't have work the next day. However, sometimes it makes more sense to have talent on a week where it's just an average weekend and not every other club in town has talent as well, because then you're not competing with anybody. For example, let's say it's Grammy weekend, and every club has a big artist performing. Do you spend the money to have someone that week when you know that you're competing with some of the bigger names, or do you save it for the following week when nobody has talent, and you're guaranteed to be the main attraction that night? It could be as strategic as that.

I have people who help me with talent buying and such. I also encourage the promoters to use their networks and reach out to different brands that may want to host parties as well. Sometimes you can get great events without spending money. We have a Scout Modeling agency holiday party coming up, for example. The models are coming for a cocktail hour before we open, and then we're going to open up and have this modeling agency party that we can then turn to the promoters to push. It's called a layered event. It really didn't cost us any money. That's why at Doheny Room, I prefer doing things that don't have a price tag associated with them.

As far as the celebrity host and that stuff, that's a little bit outdated to me. It's something that people would do in Vegas more because it's such a touristy kind of destination. Vegas is probably eighty percent tourist and twenty percent local. Whereas here, we're the opposite: we're probably eighty percent local, twenty percent tourists. When they are tourists in Vegas, they might be excited that Khloé Kardashian is hosting at someplace, and they might get to see her. That shit wouldn't fly here. It would still be somewhat of a draw here in LA, but it wouldn't be worth paying her what Vegas pays her, which would probably be something crazy like one hundred thousand dollars. They'd be able to make it back because they sell tickets for entrance and this and that. It's a different model.

Regarding music programming, Doheny Room in particular was something special because when we went to open it, we already had Hyde and Nightingale. We had to do something a little bit different, not just the same LA usual format, the same hip-hop. I wanted to elevate it and make it really diverse with different genres and throwbacks. I wanted it almost like the dancing feel you see at a wedding, but a wedding where the couple has really good taste in music, so that older people can feel comfortable going in there. We have that natural dance floor area in there, so you can't be playing only Migos. No one's going to really dance to Migos. You bop your head at your table, but you want to hear artists like David Bowie, Missy Elliot, Whitney Houston, and George Michael— people you're going to really groove to and that girls will like. That was kind of the idea behind it.

I have a good relationship with a lot of the DJs. I gave a lot of them their first gig, and I helped them mold their careers, like Devin Lucien, Bobby French, DJ Politik, and Bee Fowl. Bee Fowl even started off as my lighting tech at Voyeur, and now he's considered one of the best club DJs in LA. All these guys look at me like I was someone who really helped kick-start their careers because I gave them their gigs, and we talk music all the time. The music is really the lifeline of your experience, and if it's off, you can have a terrible time and don't even really know why you're having a bad time. The reverse could also be true. If the DJ is on point, you could be having fun and don't even know why, but it's the rhythm and flow that creates the vibe and energy for the ideal party.

Describe the general components of a nightlife marketing plan. What goes into promoting the nightclub experience, and how do Doheny Room, Nightingale, and Hyde Sunset constantly build buzz and evolve to stay relevant?

The general components of a nightlife marketing plan include a few major different parts. First and foremost, the promoters. They are the ones who are bringing bodies to the door and delivering clients, which raises the revenue. Second, traditional marketing, which includes any ads you may run. We don't invest in traditional marketing too heavily because it's not something we focus on in nightlife. That's more for restaurants and hotels. But you do have to make sure your digital footprint is on point and have good SEO (search engine optimization) and digital funnels that drive business. Third, there's public relations, which involves getting mentions and sightings and special events. Another aspect of a nightlife marketing plan is internal host programs, which is having people who are in-house whose main objective is to drive business through customer development. For instance, people who are on a program to go meet with concierges at different hotels and funnel the transient business from the twenty percent of tourists who are coming into town.

In terms of building buzz, that's where the components of social media and content are significant in the marketing plan. For example, we make recap videos of big nights where we do have a performance. We'll show the venue in full throttle and people dancing and "cheers-ing," and the video will encapsulate the entire experience within a short fifteen-second or sixty-second montage with music. Those clips help keep us relevant and show off the experience to people who may not have been able to be there or are wondering what a night there is like for the future.

Another aspect to touch on with social media is the imagery that you use. The imagery that you choose to associate with your brand affects the optics of the brand. If you look at all our Instagrams for Hyde Sunset, Doheny Room, and Nightingale, our strategy with them was, "Let's just post really cool images and have some sort of direction as far as the way that we're going." Hyde's is a little bit Old Hollywood, Doheny's is funkier and more flavorful, and Nightingale's got this kind of retro-futuristic vibe. You have some sort of direction, but just post cool images like you're a lifestyle brand.

Some places post flyer after flyer, and it's just like, "Who's going to fucking follow that?" The whole point is to get people to follow it. I'll follow a cool Instagram that just has dope videos, and I don't know who's behind it, but I'll follow it because I want to see it in my feed. It's all about a dope image and clever caption, but not even being too pitchy because people don't want to get sold to. They want to discover it. People are so inundated with all these marketers. It's almost like you have to kind of anti-market in order to be the cool place. In doing so, all of a sudden, someone decides to follow Doheny Room, and they're scrolling through their phone, and they're like, "Whoa. This is a dope image." They don't even know who posted it. Then they look and say, "Oh, Doheny Room posted this. Oh, it's Friday. Oh, maybe I should go to Doheny Room." You hook them not by posting a flyer or something that's too salesy, but just by covertly capturing their business or at least capturing their attention and then hopefully getting their business.

How has social media affected nightlife marketing?

I could write a thesis on how social media has affected nightlife. I mean, it's crazy. There are so many layers to it, and there are positives and negatives. Social media has definitely affected it. Even just from a privacy angle; I was just out the other night, and Owen Wilson was at the table close to us. Some stupid girls were Instagramming and videoing themselves, and he was mortified and didn't want to be on their Instagram. Everyone becomes a paparazzi, essentially with their phones. In that sense, I think it's made it so that bigger names are much less inclined to go out just because they don't want to deal with drunken people with their cameras and social media.

One key positive of social media is that now all the people who are in your venue are letting everybody know that they're there. You get all these people who are now your promoters for the space because they show how fun it is and make people have FOMO (fear of missing out) if they're not there. Then maybe there's a residual effect, and the following week their friends will go out because they're like, "Oh, that looked like so much fun." At the same time, it's much easier for promoters to build their network without having to go meet people organically. They can just build their network by meeting people digitally. From the promotional standpoint, it's a positive because promoters used to have to text or call all their people individually, or do an email blast or whatever to engage them, and now they just post on their story, "Pull up." Whatever. However, it's also a negative in some ways because I think social media has made some promoters a little lazy, to be honest, because they can reach all their people in a couple of posts, and they're not doing the individual outreach. I think it has also made the partygoer kind of disengaged because they're inundated with a bunch of different invites and options. The personal touch isn't quite there all the time through social media.

With buyers and clients, before, the formula was that you go to the club and spend three to five thousand dollars, and the light shows and bottles come your way, which draws the attention of the girls or whomever you want to impress. Then you're looked upon as this guy who's the hotshot, and that's maybe how you get introduced to girls or whoever. Nowadays, you can literally slide into anybody's direct messages, and you don't have to spend all that money. You can do a trip and be like, "Do you want to go on my jet?" Clients have been spending less money too because bottle service is a little bit of an archaic way to impress people. People will still go out, but they aren't dropping as much money. Now, there are more options of places to go out to every night; it's not like when it was the one it spot. The value of tables was so much more.

At the same time, girls are now so much more self-conscious and aware of where they are every night because people document their lives. If you're at the same clubs every single week, and you're going out, your friends may frown upon that or look at you as this party person, so those girls are less inclined to go out. Also, everyone's now much more health conscious because they feel they have to post their bodies on social media and would rather be posting themselves up early doing yoga and a smoothie than at the after party. It's a good thing because I guess people are being healthier and taking care of themselves more, but for nightlife, it might detract people or the influencer girls from going out all the time.

What is different about Los Angeles nightlife culture versus other party destinations, such as Las Vegas, Miami, and New York City?

I think LA's unique in the sense that you have a lot of people who come and try to take their brands to LA. Some do well if they incorporate the LA locals, and the others who don't will end up failing because it's such a niche market. It's very promoter heavy and promoter driven, so you need the right people behind you pushing the venues. Whereas a place like Vegas, it's really about the DJs and about your talent because that's what drives the bodies for the most part. For example, let's say you opened a place in Vegas, and you were partners with a DJ company—some Swedish House Mafia guys or whatever. If they were able to book DJs and talent that the other venues couldn't or didn't have access to, you could potentially succeed because it's more about battling on those terms.

For New York City, I know you have places that have lasted a long time. I think there's a lot less turnover because there are some strong operators out there that have a real foothold on the market. There are also so many people in New York, so you have millions of people on a small island to fill up a venue. You also have Wall Street and finance guys who keep you afloat. You can open up a cool bar, and it'll do well without promoters, but it's not necessarily going to be the bottle-buying success that bigger clubs see. I think it's similar in Miami—all the different cities have certain operators that kind of dictate and corner the market in some ways.

How do you make sure that your promoters represent your brands as well as you do?

Currently, we have a unique system where we have some guys who have been around for a long time who are partners within SBE nightlife and are exclusive to us. There's a team of us that really holds down the fort and leads the group. The Alliance—Josh Richman, Hartwell, and Frankie Delgado—whom I mentioned before are seasoned veterans that are still part of the team. Frankie Delgado, Josh Richman, and Hartwell, along with Dean May and Deborah Maguire, are also nightlife partners of ours and contribute heavily to the overall success of the nightlife department.

Then we have the younger kids, and some of them are really great at what they do. The older partners help groom the younger generation. It's a matter of finding talent, identifying talent, and identifying the people who you want to represent your brand and who you want to be out there pushing the venues. It comes down to their work ethic, taste, and the way they do outreach and attract people. Then we just make sure that they're on top of it, and that they're consistent and not slacking, getting into bad habits, getting caught up in drugs or all the above. See, with promoters I feel like you have to teach them to be a triple threat. First, they need to bring an attractive cool crowd. Second, they have to bring revenue in through clients. Third, they should strive to bring celebrities as well that are going to get us notoriety and build the cache of the brand.

Do you think that with the rise of feminism, the nightlife industry will ever become less male driven?

I think nightlife is already somewhat female driven in nature. Although a majority of promoters may be male, a major part of the formula is the female guests who attend parties, and the bottle service staff and the host staff who help drive business are predominately female. Hyde and Doheny Room have female general managers. Our lead designer of the latest remodel we're doing is female and so on. End of the day nightlife tends to cater most to females and their tastes and desires from the music to decor. For example, girls come in packs to Doheny Room together without promoters bringing them. Why? Because they can dance, and they can go to the bar and get their own drinks. They don't need to be at a table. They feel comfortable, and there's a feminine touch to the experience overall.

For the next generation of twenty-one-year-olds, what do you think the nightlife industry will look like, and how would you show them the ropes?

Considering the millennial appetite for constant consumption of the next and new, I've been genuinely surprised with how many venues and brands have lasted so long and have remained supported in the past five to ten years in nightlife. The model used to be that each club would have a two- to three-year shelf life, and then the space needed to be renamed and rebranded and remodeled. The loyalty I've witnessed with the younger generation has been cool to see. For the future, I think technology will start to integrate itself more within the experience, I think more creative ways to share your night out on social platforms will arise. Perhaps there could be opportunities to monetize a nightlife experience or for the influential partygoer or promoter to be compensated through brand sponsorship or other affiliates. I have some *Black Mirror* futuristic ideas in mind, where parties become manufactured due to the spread of AI and widening income inequality, but I'll save that for another conversation. To answer your question, I think there is an internal kind of need for real human connection that's lacking in this younger generation. It's due to their constant relationship with technology and always being behind a screen. I went to the Lakers game, and there's a kid playing *NBA2K* on his phone at a Lakers game watching the real thing. Amazon's making it so there's going to be no more retail or malls. I used to go to the mall when I was a kid and hang out. Now, kids don't gather like this as much face to face. You can get DoorDash or Uber Eats every day, date through a profile and text messages. The only places where people meet up and interact is at sporting events, concerts, and the club. For two of those, ultimately it's the love of music and the social energy that draws people in, and that is never going to die. That's something that's human in nature and hopefully still proves to be the case down the road.

Frankie Delgado

"I'm targeting celebrities, models, and bottle-service clients because that's
what's paying the bills."

Please enjoy learning more through my conversation with Frankie.

How did you get started in the nightlife industry? What made you want to work in nightlife?

In my heart, I always knew that I liked to throw parties. I threw my high school parties, and then when I went to college, I started throwing spring break parties, and I just started getting creative with certain things because I lived in Tijuana at the time.

I went to San Diego State and crossed the border to school, and I would bus people down to Tijuana and party out there. It was the start of me wanting to continue this as a career. Then, I partied in LA a few times with my friends from Tijuana, and I loved the way nightlife used to be—the exclusivity, the amount of people begging me to get inside the club. It felt like there was a lot of power at the door and a lot of people needed you, in a sense. I just loved that.

How many venues are you involved in now?

I work for a bigger hospitality group called SBE, and I kind of oversee a lot of things within the company, not just clubs. We have some restaurants, especially in LA, that I help out with their marketing, with their influencer programs, and making sure that the places are maintaining that cool factor. There are restaurants, hotels, any of their bars, lounges, and clubs. SBE is a little bit of everything. Within that, there are about ten properties that I oversee.

Describe your day-to-day and night-to-night responsibilities as a nightlife managing partner for SBE.

The daytime is getting stuff done for the nighttime. It's not like you have the daytime completely free, and you go to work at night. I think at night it's just the product of what you worked on during the day. During the day, I could be having my marketing meetings, my promotional team meetings, or investor meetings, or I'm reviewing the numbers that we did last week and how we can improve. It's never good enough, and it feels new every day because you have to start over every single night when it comes to clubs. Work like it is your last party—that kind of thing. I think that during the day, it's more about meetings and making sure everything goes right. Making sure the managers are doing what they're supposed to do and your promotional team is doing what they're supposed to do. Making sure the venue always looks good, and everyone's up to par, and we have events planned. It's just a lot of meetings with people to make sure that everything is always good.

Every day could change. Sometimes there's nothing to do and sometimes there are too many things to do in one day. It's also just keeping up with relationships and making sure you have layered events for your nights and your nightly promotion. Putting a layer on top of the promotional team, so they can promote somebody's birthday or somebody performing at night. It's a lot of little things that go into the day-to-day.

At night, it's making sure that everyone's balancing the room between the promoters and bottle-servers' buyers, and making sure that if there are celebrities coming, they're taken care of. It's also important that the DJ is playing the right music. I think it's a lot easier during the night than during the day, keeping up with all the clientele and the meetings and stuff.

What is different about Los Angeles nightlife culture versus other party destinations, such as Las Vegas, Miami, and New York City?

Well, it's plain and simple. There are a lot of celebrities here and a lot of companies that want to throw parties and events, and now with these influencers all over the place, there's a lot more stuff going on. Companies like to throw parties here because they know they'll get good press out of it.

Describe the general components of a nightlife marketing plan. What goes into promoting the nightclub experience, and how does Hyde Sunset constantly build buzz and evolve to stay relevant?

Once you meet that cool factor, I think you try to use it a lot and you make sure you start with the venue. For example, location. Hyde Sunset is on Sunset Boulevard in Crescent Heights, which is one of the most traffic-heavy streets in the city, and everyone goes by there to see if they can spot celebrities.

It starts there, and then who's going to run the place. Let's say I'm running the place. I have my contacts and cool people whom I can reach out to, so things spread by word of mouth: "Oh, Frankie is opening a new place, and it's going to be cool. It's going to open up Friday night." Everybody starts hitting me up, and they can now reach me through social media too. Everyone is reachable at this point.

How has social media affected nightlife marketing?

There are good promoters in the city who are going to be able to deliver the right crowd to the space, including all the influencers, celebrities, bottle clients, and lots of models and girls. With that said, when we have the right place and the right night, and it's brand-new, people start posting, "Oh, I'm here at the club," or whatever. Social media blows you up a little more, so when people come to town to visit and vacation here, they hear about the club, and they now want to come. Social media has affected nightlife, but at the same time, it's helped nightlife. There are a lot of celebrities whom we want to come out, but they can't afford to club and have a great time and enjoy the night without being bothered by someone who wants to take a picture with a celebrity. Back in the day, nobody carried their camera. I mean, they did in their pockets, but who cares? So before, maybe somebody just wanted to give a celebrity a handshake, and that was it. The celebrity could continue to drink and act wild, and there were no pictures of them doing that.

Now, everyone's taking pictures and videos, and the culture's completely different from years ago. Social media has blown up your place because it lets the masses know that this exists, so you get more hype for a longer period of time. Places used to be open for one year, and then they would shut down and be remodeled with different names so that you could continue to stay relevant. Today, clubs are lasting longer because social media is helping the club remain cool as long as people are still going.

For example, let's say, my friend, Rudy Mancuso, is at the club with his girlfriend, Maia Mitchell, and they're sitting there, take a picture together, and tag that they're at Hyde Sunset. It then goes to their mass following. Their followers now think, "Oh, they're at Hyde. The club Hyde Sunset must be cool because they are there." When people are posting inside the club and tagging us, it's great promotion on our end. Some of that is sometimes strategic, and sometimes they do it on their own. It just depends. Some people don't mind being filmed or posting on social media, but others don't want to be.

How do you cater differently to celebrities versus regular clients?

It's a case-by-case basis every single night. It just depends on how many clients we have, celebrities who come, and promoters I have that night. Sometimes, I have to combine people from other tables because there are so many tables. Sometimes a celebrity shows up, and I'd never move a client who's buying bottles, but I'm always going to strategically place promoters whom I can tell, "Hey, get up. Move. Go join another promoter because I need this table now, because Michael B. Jordan just showed up."

We move people who work for us, not people who are paying. Same with the celebrities—I would never move the celebrity. I would move another person to sit at a table that wants to spend money. You want to make sure that when you're moving people, you're not disrespecting their tables. It's more about the promotional value later on in life, and making sure you're not going to piss them off because they're not going to want to come back to your place.

What previous professional experiences have helped you most in this role?

I think that it is a natural thing, but I really think going to school, being social, and always wanting to go out. I loved partying. I loved school and throwing parties. I think I would consider myself the life of the party because you can't be boring when throwing these parties, and you have to make sure that you're enjoyable to be around. There's no room for arrogance and being mean nowadays.

Back in the day, there was more room to be arrogant, and you didn't have to let in everyone—you could be pickier back then because there were fewer clubs, fewer people, and more demand. Now there are more clubs, and they are spread out. Everybody can get in the clubs pretty much if you are dressed nicely. It's a little bit different nowadays. If you just have a good attitude and you're fun—I think that's what you need to be a part of this business. You also need to take into consideration that if you're going to do what I do, then you need to understand the value of what you're doing. I think you definitely need to have a little bit of education and a little bit of fun in you. You have to understand the money that's coming in, how much you pay promoters, etc. You're on budgets, and you have to understand numbers.

How do you hire and train your promoters?

I try to train them myself. I don't like to work with promotional clubs and stuff. I like to work with guys who work only with me. If they work somewhere else, it doesn't make sense for me.

I like to check up on my promoters and ensure they are working every day and understand the value of relationships and the kind of people I want in the club. I'm targeting celebrities, models, and bottle-service clients because that's what's paying the bills. In my opinion, I think that's what LA nightlife is.

How has your nightlife lifestyle changed since the first rendition of *The Hills*?

As seen in *The Hills: New Beginnings,* it's a little different. We are all a little bit more grown-up now. Brody Jenner and I were twenty-five and twenty-seven, respectively, when we were shooting that show. Now we're thirty-five and thirty-seven, which is a little different. There's more responsibility for me in these places now than there used to be.

How has working in the nightlife industry affected your own social life (sacrifices, trade-offs, access, etc.)?

I was able to balance my world. I always wanted to have a family, and I wanted to have a wife, and relationships outside of nightlife. I have my friendships, family time, and my work. It's difficult, but I can balance them.

For the next generation of twenty-one-year-olds, how would you show them the ropes to the nightlife industry?

You have to love the industry, partying, being creative in the building, and living during the nighttime. There's really no secret behind it. You have to have relationships and build relationships with people. A lot of people can start like I did. I started throwing parties in Tijuana and Cabo for spring break during college, but that had nothing to do with LA nightlife. Once I left Tijuana, I literally started from scratch. I just had the passion for clubs, and deciding who came in and who didn't, and where people were sat in the club. I understood that certain people sit at the better tables, and certain people didn't sit at the better tables. I understood how the room should flow, what the DJ was going to play that night, the choice of music the crowd was catering to—all that. I loved it. You have to love that.

Most people have to start at the bottom, and I started at the bottom. When I moved to LA, I didn't come with any money, so I had to get a job. I was helping out the bartenders and waitresses at client tables, and I became good at it. I then started helping the managers in the office during the daytime. As I was learning it all, little by little my relationships started becoming more relevant to LA nightlife, and I was able to say, "Hey, can I work? Let me bring some people for you to the club." It felt right. Once I had access to the club, people started hitting me up to let them in the club, and I guess that's how you get involved. From that point on, it's how deep you want to get into the industry and how many years you want to put into it. Do you have the passion? I want to design my clubs when I open them, so I was part of Hyde and Nightingale. Places that I'm going to open, I want to be part of refining them and building the promotional teams and building the essence of the club. Is it just going to be a bar where you go get a drink from 6:00 to 10:00 p.m., or is it a whole big party—what's the experience? I love that, all that. You've got to have the passion to want to do it and then build relationships, so you can get involved.

The first questions I'm going to ask anyone who wants to work with me are, Why would I hire you? What do you bring to the table?

I got a direct message the other day from a kid that works at another club, and he asked to come work for me. My response to him was, "Actually, no. I don't really want you to work. I don't really like working with people who work at other clubs." And they respond, "Why?" but in my head I'm like, "Why would I let you come into my club and come steal my clientele or go talk to my clients? Why would I trust you? All you're going to get is exposure to my friends, my people, my celebrities, my clients, my models of my club, and you're going to try to take them to another club the next day." I have about ten guys who work for me at Hyde, and they don't work anywhere else—no other nightclubs. That's just my personal preference. I give them all a home and security. I make sure they're taken care of from my side, so I can get the same back from them.

CHAPTER 4:
NEW YORK CITY—
DANIEL OLARTE REINA

"None of us are real celebrities, but we have to sell ourselves like we are."

New York City is the quintessential example of a city that has experienced a true evolution of nightlife. Although a child of the twenty-first century, I have always adored the rich history of New York institutions, such as Studio 54. Two of the biggest differences I see in New York City nightlife compared to other major metropolitan cities are smaller venue size due to apparent lack of space and high rent and the experience NYC partygoers desire. It seems that NYC partygoers are not looking for as much change and novelty as other cities but rather appreciate the tradition behind such venues. I find that partygoers in LA, Miami, and some other cities are continuously looking for something new and expect new places to pop up more frequently. Nightlife venues struggle to have longevity because the industry is all about staying trendy and relevant, but many of NYC's nightlife spots have stood the test of time.

I was thrilled to talk to Daniel Olarte Reina, who has been in the NYC nightlife scene for years and is one of the most business-savvy promoters I have ever met. Some lower-level promoters may garner a bad rap for being sleazy and annoying, but the professional ones are truly an integral part of the nightlife business. They bring cool people to the clubs in ways a flyer or social media post cannot, and then they entertain the people they bring in. They are part of the magic of the business, creating memorable nights for all partygoers. Nightlife promotion is a different type of client-facing hospitality because they form a different relationship with you than a bartender or waiter would. Promoters, especially when you are young and new to nightlife, pop bottles with you as if they are your new best friend and show you how to get the most out of your night out. Promoting also seems, in my opinion, to be the best way to learn the ropes of operating a nightclub, so it is a great gig for young people.

One of the only legitimate promotion companies based in NYC is 1990 Group. Daniel and his partners created 1990 Group to help nightlife groups better curate their guest lists and fill rooms with the right people every night. By *right people*, I do not just mean people who will spend money, but rather the partygoers who will genuinely have a good time and will return again. Daniel has spent years building 1990 Group and successfully promoting for prominent nightlife groups and clubs, such as TAO Group, The Butter Group, Bagatelle, GoldBar, and many other venues—every night of the week and multiple venues per night!

Daniel is another example of taking his passion straight from the college classroom at NYU and transferring his partying expertise to the real world, projecting the profitable future of the nightlife industry. Although Daniel was able to apply his expertise in promotional services in an array of jobs, he recognized his natural talent for nightlife promoting. I admire that Daniel is able to showcase nightlife experiences to a variety of crowds and is adamant in attempting to meet people's high expectations when going out. He is aware of the power of strategizing the right crowd for the right party. He takes advantage of NYC being a major tourist destination and helps both tourists and locals enjoy incredible NYC experiences without a hefty price tag. Furthermore, Daniel does not just guide people to superb parties; he encourages people to interact and connect as well. Some of the most memorable nights out are due to whom you are with and whom you meet.

Coming from the competitive background of banking, it is no surprise that Daniel has been incredibly successful in NYC's competitive nightlife scene. I loved hearing how he and 1990 Group's mission goes far beyond just promoting nightclubs and partying; it is bringing people of all (legal) ages and industries together to participate in the memorable nights inside these venues. Daniel and his team truly care about the partygoers' experiences as much as they care about doing a solid job for the venues, and for that I really admire them.

Please enjoy learning more through my conversation with Daniel.

Describe the 1990 Group and the promoting team.

The 1990 Group is a Spanish company based in New York. Half of the team is from Spain, and the other half is from all over the world: Denmark, Serbia, Colombia, and Venezuela. We're really diverse, which is a good thing because we can bring different kinds of people to the clubs. Right now we have about twenty-five to thirty people on our team, and everyone does different things within the team. We create small groups, usually two or three guys in each, based on their ages, personalities, and networks. It's more effective and efficient to work in groups.

In the beginning, 1990 Group started with only nightlife. We were just a nightclub promoter group. Back in the day when I was at New York University, I used to bring all the New York students to the clubs with 1990 Group. Over time, more venues, restaurants, organizations, and schools saw the potential of our company.

Nonprofit organizations started to hire us because they wanted us to bring a specific group of people. We go through our data and see who will be interested in going to their event. For the organization, it is important for us to show them that we will get people to pay for a ticket or donate while proving that we are thinking not only about the money but also of people who will be involved with the cause long term.

During the summertime, a lot of international students come to New York City for internships, especially for banks like JP Morgan, Deutsche Bank, and Bank of America. They do summer programs and bring people from all over the world to New York. The students are only here for two to three months, so their goal is to work hard and play hard. We try to target those people and create specific experiences for them. For example, we try to get them a good deal in which they can come to a venue for a less expensive price and get the best experience. We also do things like summer cruises, so they can see the city on a cruise, have a couple of drinks, party a little bit, and do a little networking. A lot of these people come here because they want to explore New York City, but they also want to network and connect with the locals. Sometimes there is matchmaking in this business too. Sometimes it happens that we introduce two people, and then they come back to us saying, "Remember you introduced us a few years ago? Now we're engaged" or, "I met this person through you when I was looking for a job, and I got a job."

Our high season is summertime, especially at the end of the summer, and the lowest season for us is probably January or February because it's cold in New York. Those are usually the months that we let people on our team go home, take a few weeks off, and take it easy. It's the time to recover because you have the rest of the year to be a little tenser. March is when it starts picking up strength again. The weather gets better, and then people get a little bit excited and want to go out more.

How did you get started in the nightlife industry? What made you want to work in nightlife?

To be honest, when we started 1990 Group almost eight years ago, it was completely different. Now, it's more professionally structured. Back then, we were four people. It was my brother, my father, Ricardo, and Victor. At that time, I was starting to do my master's degree at NYU, and my brother had just graduated. He had also been working for SFX Entertainment, which owns major festivals around the world, including Tomorrowland, TomorrowWorld, and Electric Zoo. The other two guys, Ricardo and Victor, were students back then. They wanted to promote, so we had that connection at the time. We said, "Okay, we'll help you guys out. We'll do more of the business and administration work." We had a different goal than just promoting. For my brother, he was going to work for my dad's company, and I was to go to NYU, do my schoolwork, graduate, and then go back to banking. Back then it was more about making money, having fun, bringing out small groups of friends, and getting paid for it. Little by little it grew, and venues started asking us for more promoters and had more clubs that they wanted us to work at.

As time passed, we realized that there was a lot of potential in the industry and demand for our services. We saw the potential mainly because part of my family does real estate development. They build hotels, nightclubs, restaurants, and entertainment complexes. I realized that my brother and I were the only ones in the family focusing on the entertainment side. We figured we could create a company that would hopefully one day contribute to the family business on the entertainment side and would be able to fulfill my family business gap. Instead of hiring people from outside companies to run the venues inside properties, we could provide the services.

People don't see nightlife as a real industry and promoting as a career. Some people see it more as a temporary thing that you can do while you go to school to have fun, making some money while you work or study. But in reality, there is a lot of potential. Nightlife and promotion is still growing. It needs to be more standardized, and we're trying to fill that gap in the industry and in New York City. The nightclub industry is also growing, and nightlife groups are expanding. All the renowned brands, such as 1OAK and Marquee, are opening everywhere—Europe, Asia, and other places in North America. As they expand, we can expand with them. Promoting teams exist in different places like Miami, LA, and Vegas, but they are not as big as us. We are probably the biggest promoting team company in the United States, and we are probably the most competitive in the industry at the moment because everything is competitive in New York City no matter what industry you're in.

Describe your day-to-day and night-to-night responsibilities as a promoter for 1990 Group.

Being a promoter is not only being a promoter. In Spain, they just call it PR, public relations. Promoting involves marketing, PR, advertising, and a bit of management. People believe that you can just go out, have a good time, and get paid for it, but they don't know all the things that we do during the day—all the meetings, interviews, and business development that we have to do on a daily basis. We have people who are in the office all day, so from 9:00 in the morning to 6:00 p.m. while the promoters go out at night. The promoters cannot really wake up early in the morning, so that's why we have other employees there during the day. The promoters come to the office around 2:00–3:00 p.m., but we only have until 5:00 p.m. to deal with business development during business hours. If we want to call all the clients or banks or whatever, it has to be done before 5:00 p.m. We understand that they don't care about our schedule. For that reason, we have somebody here during the day working, and they don't really go out at night as a promoter.

We have different night-to-night responsibilities for the venues. Our main job is to bring people. Most of us at 1990 Group are mass promoters, so we help bring a lot of bodies to the venues on days that they're open. Not many people want to go out Monday through Wednesday, so we help fill the venue and make it look fun on those days.

Our second job is to bring clients who buy tables or bottles, but it's not a must. We don't have to bring clients because that's not what we get hired for, but it helps us become more relevant to the venues. For example, when there's a big event, and they are choosing which promoters to have, that's one of the factors that they take into account. You want to be the promoter who brings a lot of bodies but also brings a lot of money to the venue. Money comes from people buying bottles, bar tabs, and covers. For example, if we bring two hundred people to the venue one night, maybe we don't have anyone buying a table, but out of the two hundred people, let's say fifty or one hundred people pay cover. Each cover is fifty dollars. Do the math. That's a lot of money for the venue. With that money we create, they can pay us and make a profit from the crowd we bring.

How has the 1990 Group team been able to make promoting a career rather than just a side hustle?

We are lucky because promoters working individually don't have the help of a team like we do, and in my opinion, it's the only way we've been able to grow as much as we have. When you have a team, you are supported. There are days that you are slow or you're not performing as well as you're supposed to, but then you have your team that can help you out.

Describe the general components of a nightlife marketing plan. What goes into promoting the nightclub experience, and how do you help your clients constantly build buzz and evolve to stay relevant?

When it comes to marketing for a nightclub or any venue in nightlife, there are three main components. First, nightclubs usually use social media, flyers, and online advertising for marketing their general programming. Second, a widely used marketing tactic is bringing a performer. A performer is not going to cost the club too much. They are going to cost the club probably five to twenty thousand dollars. With this performer, the contract they sign says that they will sing probably four to five songs, and that will be part of the performance of the night. That makes more sense sometimes because it's not as expensive as hiring big-name DJs like Tiesto, who could cost around one hundred thousand dollars. You still get what you were looking for, which is a performance of the few famous songs that they have, and you get a lot of big spenders buying tables and bottles. Those nights are good, but the clubs have to be really picky because they can't bring the same performer every two weeks. It becomes boring, so they always look for the right performer and right time. What they often do is hire performers who are already in the city because then the club doesn't have to pay for the hotels or transportation. They simply pay for performers to come to the club, sing four songs, be there for thirty to forty minutes, and that's it.

The third marketing option is where we come into play as promoters. This is the best way to promote a venue because it's the cheapest way. The reason they hire us is to bring people who are really fun, energetic, and good-looking. I will say this is the option used about eighty percent of the time in the industry. People will go to a club because of the DJ, performer, or promoter. If someone has a group of twenty people they want to go to a club with, but they don't want to spend thirty or forty thousand dollars on a table or bottles, they reach out to a promoter. They tell their friends, "Let me talk to this promoter who can help me out on discounts for the guys, getting the girls for free, and getting unlimited drinks all night." A promoter will then help them with the nightclub experience—having a good time with good music and being surrounded by fun people.

How important is it for nightclub promoters to be active on social media?

Before social media, it was pretty much all word of mouth. Nowadays, it's all about social media. When I started promoting ten years ago, I didn't even have an Instagram, but I had a lot of contacts. I just knew a lot of people. Now, social media is kind of your face. It's your résumé. If people are following you, they want to party with you because of who you are, your lifestyle, the places you go to, etc. Your social media has to reflect that. However, you can sell the best party ever on social media, but it's not until the partygoers go out with a promoter and experience nightlife that they are convinced that nightclubs are fun. Then they're like, "Wow, this is actually really good," and if they see the service that we provide, they're like, "Oh my god, Daniel, we appreciate all your help." Next time, maybe they will want a night out in the city with all their friends, and they are comfortable reaching out to us because they know we will hook them up. Customer loyalty is necessary in every business.

Social media is an amazing tool because you can advertise. You can target people now on Facebook because all these social media platforms offer great tools for marketing. For example, if I want to do an event and target people between twenty-one and thirty-five who are living in the Lower East Side and are professionals, I can target all these things on Facebook and Instagram and pay for a little package to get a bunch of impressions on Facebook and Instagram. I don't do this really, to be honest, but I've seen people who even target me. They send me messages on social media saying, "I'm going out tonight," or sometimes I'll reach out to people about special events, but I could see why people get annoyed from all the messages that promoters sometimes send out. I understand if you know the person, but if you don't know the person, they're like, "Why are you sending this information?" It's part of the job in a way, but privacy and data are current issues for social media. Promoters need to find the right balance of targeting and advertising, but not in a creepy way.

If you don't focus on social media, you're not going to be relevant for this generation. I think it's good to hold back a little with posting, though, because it leaves some mystery and incentive for people to go out and see what nightlife is for themselves. I think some venues put too much out there, and I feel like I experienced the whole night without even going. Sometimes partygoers are so overwhelmed with information, marketing, PR, and flyers that they don't know where to go. I don't want 1990 Group to just be part of the clutter. Social media is definitely a tool we have to use, but it's important that we learn how to use them effectively. I'm actually working on an app right now related to nightlife because I think apps are also part of future nightlife promotion.

What is different about New York City nightlife culture versus other party destinations, such as Las Vegas, Miami, and Los Angeles?

Las Vegas is mainly tourists and definitely an older crowd. People going to Vegas are specifically going to spend money at the casinos, hotels, nightclubs, and restaurants. People have high standards for nightlife because they are specifically going for the parties and to show off at these venues. Since the masses are going to Vegas, it's not as exclusive. Everyone usually gets into the club if they pay cover or buy a table.

At the clubs in New York City, not everyone gets in. Even if they let you in, you may have to pay cover. New York is more exclusive, high-end, and VIP. It's a smaller scene. People who walk into clubs in New York City are either cool or have connections.

Miami has a different kind of energy. In Miami, you see a lot of young people because there are a lot of universities. Also, the weather is better, and there is the beach, so people don't go to Miami only for the clubs. Nightlife is not the main purpose.

What are the biggest challenges of working in nightlife promotion?

One part of the challenge is scheduling. We work different schedules than people in most other industries. Your regular promoter will work from 11:00 p.m. to 4:00 p.m. When it comes to the people who are running the promoting teams like me or managers from the nightclubs, we have to also work during the day to get organized in the office and talk to managers, lawyers, and everyone else who works nine-to-five jobs.

Another challenge is that the nightlife promotion industry is not structured. Nightlife and promoting are technically two different industries. As promoters, we have to figure out ways we can be more relevant and make people want to party with us. As a venue, they have to get people to want to party there. How can we both bring more people, more clients, and more money to this place? For promoters, how can we have people come and party with us instead of another promoter or promoter team? What do we offer that's different than everyone else? We need to think about all these things. We need to think about our target market. What kind of people should we bring to the club? People have different ways they like to party, so it is our job to figure out who the people are, and how we can match the needs of the people to the needs of the venues.

A third challenge is showing people that nightlife promoting is a legitimate career. Back in the day, it was more of a temporary kind of thing. You simply went to the clubs, had fun, and got paid for bringing a couple of people. But now it's a whole different animal. Now, running a business like 1990 Group, we run into similar questions as I mentioned before. What do we offer as a promoting team that nobody else does? How can we convince people to work with us instead of other promoting teams?

How does 1990 Group continuously build its clientele?

There are different factors we consider when deciding which clubs to work for. First of all, we're all working for the money, but that's not the only thing. If we get offered a good deal, we try our best to provide our service, so we can get the money of course, but there are places that are not even worth the money for different reasons. One reason is if we don't have the right contacts for the crowd that the venue is aiming to attract. For example, if there is a Russian party, and a venue wants to hire me, I personally don't have the Russian following for it. If I have somebody on our team who does, then I send them, but sometimes we don't have the right people.

Another reason we have to turn down offers from venues is because we've already accepted too many. We have contracts in place for several venues, so even though we get an offer for a higher amount of money, we still have to say no because of loyalty to these clubs. It's possible to stop working at one venue and jump to another one to give it a try. However, if we want to try promoting at a new venue and risk it, we make sure it's worth it. We've had cases where it ends up not being worth it. For example, we start working at a new place and have a contract saying that we will make a percentage of the bar and will be running the whole venue. We do it successfully for a few weeks, but then when it comes time to pay, they're like, "Oh, we're not going to pay you what we agreed on because we just don't want to, because we feel like that's a lot of money for you guys." Then we take them to court because we did our job, and they didn't fulfill their contractual promise. However, something that I learned in nightlife is that you can never make enemies. At some point in your career, you're going to work with them again. We have even worked again with some of the people we've taken to court. Overall, it's important to pick and choose whom you want to work with.

Do your clients care that you promote for other venues? Has anyone tried to make an exclusive deal with you so that you're only promoting their venues?

This is an issue that we were fighting for several years. At first, we had nightclubs saying to us, "No, you cannot work for anybody else. You have to work only for us, and we'll give you so much money." We came back with the approach of, "Listen, we're an independent company. We provide our service to the industry." Some have even thought about buying us, but then they realize all the expenses that would go along with the purchase—paying salaries, insurance, etc.

The nightlife groups want a monopoly. They want to be the only nightclubs in New York City and in the United States, and they want to have the best promoters and the best clients. But for us, diversity is what gives us the power and makes us who we are. Our job as an independent promoting company is to provide the same service to everyone in the industry. Every club has a different concept, so seeing the competition helps us be stronger and better promoters. We also have to protect ourselves because there have been times where a venue or one of the owners will be upset, and they're like, "Okay, I don't want you guys anymore," and we're like, "Wow, thank God we have other clients." Otherwise, we would be screwed. That's why we would rather stay independent and have our own policies, information, and way of doing business. We have the freedom to make our own decisions.

What do you think about the "fame" that goes along with being a nightclub promoter?

That's a great question. The thing is, none of us are real celebrities, but we have to sell ourselves like we are. Partygoers like our lifestyles. A lot of these guys who work with me were athletes or models, or they used to throw all the parties at their schools. They were group leaders and sociable, which helps us be relevant and relatable. Sometimes partygoers reach out to us for our service, and other times they just want to party with us because of who we are.

People who go out with us always say, "Oh my god, I love what you do. I would love to have your job," but they don't know what it really entails. They see us going out, partying, and drinking all the time, but they don't know what we do really. I mean, half of my team doesn't even drink, and most of our team members have girlfriends and are in stable relationships, so it's not like they're sleeping around like a lot of people think promoters do. Also, it's not like we bring our friends and get paid. We work at the office every single day, and then we still have to perform at night. We are all best friends, but when we work, we work. It's a little bit like *Entourage*, but it's also a job.

Would 1990 Group ever open its own nightclub one day?

We've thought about it so many times. I feel like everyone's dream is to own a nightclub and restaurants, but after working in the industry so long, we understand all the responsibility that comes with it. Now, you don't even need to own a nightclub and pay rent for the venue; you can just be the management company behind it. For instance, nightclubs are sometimes co-owned with hotels. The hotel's main purpose is running the hotel, but then they hire a management company to run the nightclubs, restaurants, rooftops, etc. The venues aren't the hotels' main source of revenue, but they use them to attract people to stay there.

I used to think owning a club would be an awesome thing, but with time I realized that I'd rather just be a management company. If we were to open a club, it would have to be the right concept at the right time and at the right price. You can make an enormous amount of money owning a club, but it has to be under the right conditions.

How does the drinking age in America being twenty-one affect 1990 Group's ability to bring partygoers inside the venues?

I mean, I'm Columbian, and in Columbia you have to be eighteen to go to the clubs. I think it's an issue that you have to be twenty-one or older to go to a club here because by the time you're that age, you're already into a more mature stage of your life. You have to get a job and be responsible, and you won't be able to party as much. Your life span of nightlife in America is between twenty-one to twenty-three, let's say. You are twenty-two or twenty-three when you graduate from college and start working. You still go out, but you're not going out every day, just weekends probably. In other countries, it's eighteen plus, so the lifespan of nightlife is much longer—eighteen to twenty-three, let's say. It's easier to fill a club when you have a wider age group to let in.

Also, most eighteen-year-olds in other countries have had drinks with their family and learned how to drink safely. Here in the United States, most people don't start drinking until they're twenty-one and out of their parents' house. They probably haven't been exposed to going out or drinking in a club setting, which can become dangerous. Sometimes this affects my job too because I feel responsible. I want to make sure that nobody is being taken advantage of, especially girls. If they're drinking so much that they blackout and don't know what's happening, that's dangerous. I've taken girls home or called them to make sure they're fine. I'm a little bit of a babysitter. That's also another reason why people go out with 1990 Group: because they feel comfortable. I'm not there to judge anybody, but sometimes I need to jump in for their safety.

I know the United States is a little complicated, and I don't think things are going to change. In the last few years, clubs have actually been stricter in New York. Because we're a mostly international team, we don't really know what a real ID looks like. That isn't our responsibility; it's the club security's responsibility. It's up to them to let people in or out. The clubs obviously tell us, "Be responsible. Make sure you bring the people who are over twenty-one." However, if we bring one hundred fifty people in just one night, how am I going to find out if everyone is over twenty-one? That's not part of my job.

What do you think about the nightlife industry being so male-dominated?

It is, you're right. It's interesting you say this because we recently discussed having more girls and diversity in general on our team. At the end of the day, we've hired girls, but it always ends up being a seasonal kind of thing. They come six months or one year, and they're done. Girl promoters always think that they can do a great job because they say, "Oh my god, I can bring my friends out, and it will be so easy." Now, try doing that three hundred sixty-five days a year. How many of your friends can go out every day? They see how hard it is. It's not just about bringing your friends.

This industry can be intense, and the people whom you're dealing with can be very tough. Inequality is maintained because people in the industry can speak and act aggressively, and both girls and guys can get emotional, but girls naturally tend to be a little more emotional. However, we have known girls who are amazing. We had a girl in this industry for about fifteen years. She worked by herself, and she was one of the best promoters in New York City. The reason why was because she had a really strong personality, and she didn't let anybody go over her. She was really social and nice, but when it came to work and business, she knew what she needed to do. If you're a girl with that kind of determination and persistence, it will work. She retired two years ago, and we actually bought her promotions company. She was our biggest competitor, and we were lucky that we were able to work together and invite her whole team to work with us. Apart from her, we've had all these girl promoters, but they never really last because they get emotional. I've had guys and girls come to me crying because they couldn't handle it, but it's important for me to have team members who can support me and be tough.

On the venue side, we see girls in the higher positions, such as managers, accountants, etc. Inside the clubs, the bartenders and waitresses tend to be girls because the guys are the ones who tend to buy the bottles and the tables. Most of the time, the big spender is the guy, so you want somebody from the opposite sex taking care of them. If you have a guy spending like twenty thousand dollars one night with their five guy friends, they want to have a good-looking girl bringing them their expensive bottles. In the nightlife industry, girls don't tend to go to a nightclub to spend a lot of money and buy bottles. If that was the case, trust me, you would have male waiters. The guys who are coming to the club and spending money are typically the guys in high-paying industries, such as banking. Why don't girls come to the club and spend money? It's something about the way girls think—they don't want to go to a club and spend money with their girlfriends as much as guys do. I think it is getting better because I now sometimes take out girls who just want to come, go to the bar, and buy themselves a drink. Those girls are the ones who are independent, have jobs, make enough money, and don't want to be bothered by other people. For other girls, when they have the option of turning to a promoter for free drinks, they do it.

Do the clubs lose a significant amount of money by giving promoters free tables and bottles every night?

We get the tables and bottles for free for promotional purposes because the idea is that there will be enough clients spending money each night to cover the expenses of giving us those bottles. The idea is to have a promoter like us next to a client because if we have good-looking girls dancing at our table, then the client is going to want to spend more money to impress them. So financially, that's how it makes sense.

How has working in the nightlife industry affected your own social life (sacrifices, trade-offs, access, etc.)? Do you get to have your own nights out?

When I have time off, I don't really go to a club unless I want to go to a different club that I don't work at, and I want to see what the competition is doing. It's my job to be on top of things. Although I do love going out because I'm a really social person, sometimes I just want to go to a movie, eat out, spend time with family, play sports, etc.

Who are your mentors, and why are they quality leaders?

My aunt and uncle are real estate developers who build hotels, nightclubs, and restaurants. I admire how they run their businesses as a family and team. I also look up to Jason Strauss and Noah Tepperberg, who created TAO Group. They started as a promoting company like us, and now they own several restaurants and nightclubs across the globe, such as Marquee. They are a good example of what 1990 Group can accomplish, and what they have done is amazing.

Do you request feedback from partygoers after you take them out?

The only feedback we ask for is from the nightclubs, venues, and business partners, but not from the partygoers. When I meet somebody for the first time at the nightclub, and they give me their contact information, I reach out and say, "It was nice meeting you. Hope you had a great time." If they give us the feedback, it's because they want to give it to us. It's amazing when someone comes to us at the end of the night or messages us the next day saying, "You guys are the best," or, "Thank you for everything. I really needed a fun night out." Their gratitude makes us feel good, and it's sometimes better than getting paid because I feel proud of our work and the impact we made.

For the next generation of twenty-one-year-olds, how would you show them the ropes to the nightlife industry?

I would show them where to go, give them little tricks for how to have a good time, and let them experience it for themselves. It's helpful to know which venues are popular on each day, especially if you're a tourist. I would also tell them to follow 1990 Group on social media and follow each member of my team because each person will give you a different nightlife experience. We can give people different kinds of nights out, so they can ultimately see which ones they like most. In terms of the industry, it's about teaching them the reality of the nightlife industry and telling them that it's a real career and business, not only fun.

CHAPTER 5:
BOSTON—ALYSSA MCCOURT

"I treated that night like a showcase of my talent rather than a night of partying."

Boston nightlife is known to be a bit behind the times, but this is only because it is more of a bar-heavy nightlife scene. When I worked at Royale Boston in the summer of 2017, it was evident that many of the nightclubs did not bring in big-name DJs, and the crowds were typically very international. Although I was not in the nightlife capital, I learned so much from my supervisor, Alyssa McCourt, who is a total girl boss. She was the marketing director at Royale Boston, and she truly showed me how she overcame the male dominance of the nightlife industry.

She had a vision of what the night should look like and feel like for customers, and she always achieved it. Her work ethic was diligent—she never went with the first draft of flyers from the graphic designer, she always had the energy to hand glow foam sticks to partygoers each night, and she always knew how to satisfy customers when issues occurred. Like I learned in my marketing courses, people are more likely to return to a place where something went wrong but was handled properly, rather than if nothing went wrong at all. Alyssa definitely followed that by ensuring every customer problem was addressed. She made every guy and girl walking into the club feel like a VIP, whether they seemed like they were going to buy one drink or spend thousands on a table. I am so glad I got to work with her, learn from her, and watch her throw memorable nights for guests. Currently, Alyssa works as the sales and marketing manager for Hard Rock International in Boston.

Please enjoy learning more through my conversation with Alyssa.

How did you get started in the nightlife industry?

I got my feet wet in the industry by working for BNG. I knew I was fascinated by the industry but couldn't find a way in. Los Angeles nightlife is very intense, and you really need to know someone to get in. I got invited through Instagram by some random girl to invite my girlfriends out for a free VIP table at a club called the Attic. I thought this might be a unique way to show that I am capable of creating experiences. I got as many friends as I could, which ended up being fifteen to twenty beautiful girls, and went. We stood out in the club and captured quite a bit of attention, so I found out who worked for the club and asked to speak to the marketing director. I treated that night like a showcase of my talent rather than a night of partying. I showed him my table and basically said that I wanted to work for them, and I could bring people to them every night. He told me they had an open call for jobs, and I should come by the next week. I went in and was surrounded by hundreds of the most beautiful people I had ever seen, all hoping to get a job. I finally got my turn and interviewed in the same club I had been partying at a few nights prior. I was nervous, but they liked me and told me I could intern for them.

I started interning, and after a week they offered me a position. I worked my way up in that company through a lot of networking and hard work. I went from running out for coffee and carrying food in my purse, in case my marketing director needed a snack, to running the entire private events department for the company.

What made you want to work in nightlife?

I was always fascinated by it. The big lights, beautiful people—it was a challenge to me. I liked the idea of this secret society that was so hard for people to get into, and I knew I wanted to be a part of it. There is always something new thrown your way, and the idea of having to constantly be on your toes excited me.

Describe what your day-to-day and night-to-night responsibilities were as marketing and events manager at Royale Nightclub.

I was responsible for handling all online ticketing from beginning to end. That included working with a graphic designer to create content for the website and ticket site, pricing out tickets and knowing how many to allot to each ticket type, keeping up with all current trends to keep things exciting and refreshing for incoming guests, and finding themes that worked for our nightly events. I was responsible for working with and booking DJs and other talent that we hosted in our venue, including keeping up with hospitality riders.

I managed a team of interns who would assist in building out our social media presence, and they would help oversee nightly events. I was able to double our social media presence with my team in as little as six months. I helped bring on new talent and oversaw the back-of-house production. I was responsible for coordinating with our in-house team of dancers, bottle service and VIP staff, and concert staff to make sure they had what they needed to run a successful event.

What previous professional experiences have helped you most in this role?

My experience at Jillian's in Los Angeles helped shape my career. I started as a server and eventually became the assistant to the event manager there. That job showed me the inner workings of hospitality and helped me build on my people skills. Sometimes people are so difficult, but that job really taught me how important it is to have a hospitality face, as I like to call it. That is the face when everything is going wrong and someone is upset and screaming in your face, but you are still smiling.

What were some job perks that you enjoyed?

I'd say the number of people I've gotten to meet. I've met some really famous people and gotten to have such normal moments with them, from seeing people with no makeup on to chilling on couches to partying it up with the likes of Johnny Depp, Justin Bieber, and Jennifer Lopez.

What made Royale different from a typical nightclub?

Royale became a family to me, and the venue at the time was the biggest nightclub in Boston. So it had this uniqueness to it, a place where everyone came in and was shocked. New England is not known for its nightlife scene, so a lot of times Royale was the first club at which people got that true nightlife experience. For me, that was special to be a part of someone's special night out. A lot of people would travel from northern Maine or the woods of New Hampshire just to experience it.

What is different about Boston nightlife culture versus other party destinations, such as Las Vegas, Miami, Los Angeles, and New York City?

Honestly, I'd say Boston is behind the times. Miami, Los Angeles, and Vegas are known for their nightlife, so they are always competing with other clubs right around the corner and are much more modern and bizarre. Boston is a lot more old school; they have been doing it for a long time, and it works for them. I think over the course of the next ten years, Boston nightlife is going to see some really big changes. They already have with Grand coming into town, which is going to create some competition, which will create change.

Describe the general components of a nightlife marketing plan. What goes into promoting the nightclub experience, and how did Royale constantly build buzz and evolve to stay relevant?

Royale focused heavily on social media presence; the club was really the only one of its kind for ten plus years. A lot of what helps build nightlife—and this goes for all venues, not just Royale—is experiences. Royale has a lot of really special people working for them who know how to create these. We'd start off by making a catch flyer and staying up on trends, and then we would head straight to socials. I believe in being consistent and having a dominant presence on social media, so I made sure we were posting several times a day. We would track our insights to get a better idea of when was the most optimal time to post and follow that.

I also believe it's important to interact with your guests online, good or bad. If someone had a bad time, how can we fix it? If someone had a great time, let's celebrate together! Everyone wants to be heard, and no one wants to talk to a robot, so you have to give your brand a voice and be consistent with it. What are you looking to be? Are you a cool brand, sexy brand, grungy brand? You need to find what works for you, sound like that, and transform into that. We also used marketing tools through our Wi-Fi and email to reach other guests who maybe were in our venue at the time or have never even heard of us.

Have there been measurable benefits from using social media? If so, what are they, and how have you measured them?

Yes, I'm a huge believer in social media and the power of it. My generation and the generations behind me focus so much on what's happening on their devices. They don't read newspapers or magazines, and radio is a dated tool in most cases. Don't get me wrong; these work sometimes, but I find that social media is really the best way to reach the demographic that is coming to clubs. I've tracked social media followings and interactions for any company I worked for because it's pretty hard to gain a following and stay consistent with it. I encourage people who work under me to do the same and practice on their own page. No one knows you better than yourself, so make yourself a brand and find your brand voice. It's amazing to see what you can do and small tricks you learn along the way. Luckily, Facebook and Instagram have some great tools to track your insights, which I find to be very helpful. I can view what is the best time to post and even see when something I posted isn't doing well and try to figure out why.

Who are some of your mentors, and why are they quality leaders in your eyes?

I've had some great bosses and some bad bosses, but I've learned from all of them. I'm a big fan of people watching, and it's just as important to do that in the workplace as it is in the mall. My old boss, Jamison at Royale, was probably one of my biggest mentors; he's been in the business for so long and followed a career path that I would like to follow. I'm also really intrigued by women in the industry because although from the outside it seems like it's a woman's world because beauty drives nightlife, so much of it is such a male-driven industry. I'm empowered when I see women who know what they want and don't let people push them around. I've had a few awesome lady bosses in my time who taught me never to be silenced and stand up for what you know is right.

Most leaders in the nightlife industry are men, so how did it feel being a female leader in the workplace? Were you treated differently?

Absolutely, I've been treated differently because I'm a woman my entire career. The nightlife industry for so long has capitalized on the beauty of women; when things like that happen often, women become objects or tools. Women in nightlife are taught that they are only good for their bodies, and you have to be beautiful. I've been silenced for being too aggressive or having an opinion so many times. Once I snap back at them, they typically respect me; I simply had to learn the hard way that I needed to stick up for myself. I found that my opinion was not valid and often had to make my idea seem like it was something they came up with by using a lot of wordplay.

Do you think sexism in the nightlife industry will ever evolve (no more "ladies' night," more females buying tables, bottle girls *and* boys, etc.)?

This is such a tough question that I go back and forth on. I sometimes think it's about women overcoming the suppression they feel and saying, "No more." Men need women to get into the club; ratios matter. However, I don't think there will ever be a time where there are no more bottle girls dressed scantily, because at the end of the day, sex sells. This goes beyond our nightlife industry and extends to pretty much any industry—hospitality industry, music industry, acting industry, and so on.

Women need to love themselves and find their voice, which I think is happening. It took a long time for me to find my voice, and when I did, I never stopped talking. Women need to empower each other more, especially in nightlife. They tear each other down and feed into it all. If they start uplifting each other and telling each other how good they are at their job and that their opinions might actually work, we may see a change. There is power in numbers, so come together! When I worked for a club in Los Angeles, we actually had a male bottle server, and everyone loved it. I hope to see more of that in the future.

How did working in the nightlife industry affect your own social life (sacrifices, trade-offs, access, etc.)?

I missed out on a lot of holidays with my family, never really had a true New Year's kiss, and viewed clubs in a different light than my friends. My friends wanted to go out, but when I'd join, it would feel like I'm working even if I had never even been to that club. I started analyzing the servers and bartenders, and my brain would start spinning with ideas. Oftentimes when I'd go out, it would end up being a brainstorming session for my own clubs. I would pick apart what I didn't like and what I did like and bring it back to my own work.

My family struggled with it; I missed a lot of time with my nieces and nephews when they were little. I was really lucky to have a mom who supported me and never stopped me from working; she was a big supporter in everything I did. She wanted me to experience it all. I'd say my relationships suffered the most with significant others; they hated me working in clubs. They just didn't understand it and viewed it as a party lifestyle. There was a lot of jealousy because my job required me to interact with so many people—a lot of times people with more money than they had, or what they thought was more attractive than them or better for me in their minds. I always chose my career, though, because I knew if they couldn't support me in that aspect of my life, they probably weren't the one for me.

For the next generation of twenty-one-year-olds, how would you show them the ropes to the nightlife industry?

I always try to start off by being their friend because, honestly, I wish I had more of that in the beginning of my career. The nightlife industry is full of people who are after something, whatever it may be, and it's hard to tell people's true intentions. I look out for my people and make sure they are with safe people, making choices that won't affect the rest of their lives, and most important staying true to who they are. It's easy to lose yourself in this industry.

I'd teach them the back-end stuff that no one else teaches you and things that you can't learn in school. A lot of that is watching people's body language and trying to read people. In hospitality, you have to be able to read people and adjust yourself to them because it's not about you—it's about them. If you can master that, you'll make a lot of money in this industry. I'd teach them to think about all the worst-case scenarios before making a decision. How will this affect your client? How will this affect your venue? How will this affect you? It's also important to ask questions and remind yourself that you don't know everything. I'm still learning things every day in my career. When you stop learning and think you know everything, something will go wrong, so be prepared for that.

Debonair Social Club

CHAPTER 6:

CHAPTER 6:
CHICAGO—STEVE HARRIS

"My break-the-ice, new-hire interview, go-to question: 'Can you stay up late?'"

I didn't know much about Chicago's nightlife because I only visited Chicago when my brother attended Northwestern University, and I was in my early teens. I was very appreciative to include and speak with Steve Harris, who runs Debonair Social Club. Debonair is a boutique nightclub that has been operating for more than ten years. Steve is definitely a veteran in the business and knows exactly how to throw a buzz-worthy party that celebrities and every type of Chicago partygoer will want to attend.

Please enjoy learning more through my conversation with Steve.

How did you get started in the nightlife and hospitality industries?

My good friend who worked at a downtown bar that I was always impressed with, and he asked me to pick up some shifts. It was a blast, and I ended up staying with the company for close to twenty years. Outtakes NightClub 1988, one block from the infamous Limelight.

What made you want to work in nightlife?

I have always been fond of the hospitality industry and attracted to entertainment and creative environments. My grandfather (the first Steve Harris) owned and operated venues, and I'd like to believe it skipped a generation and stuck to me. I've always preferred working nights. My break-the-ice, new-hire interview, go-to question: "Can you stay up late?"

Describe your day-to-day and night-to-night responsibilities at Debonair Social Club.

I am an operating partner in three venues, including Debonair Social Club (nightclub), Dorian's (hidden door concept, cocktail bar, restaurant with stage), and Saved by the Max LA (pop-up diner experience inspired by a 1990s TV sitcom).

Day-to-day varies with typical daytime operations to include overseeing manager meetings (including conference calls), financials, marketing, staffing, ordering, receiving, licensing, repair and maintenance vendor relations, neighbors, etc.

Night-to-night responsibilities are visiting venues (on weekends for sure) and special events. I have partners and managers that open and close each venue on given shifts. Once the venue is open, my visits are focused on observing the customers' experiences. Lights, air, music levels, and vibe are the basics to make sure people are comfortable, safe, and having fun. Notes outside of safety issues are mainly based on vibe and sales.

Always be networking with an ear out for new business.

What previous professional experiences have helped you most in this role?

Obviously, working every job role possible in a restaurant or nightclub was a ton of help. Working for a top-notch hospitality company was also huge. I consider every time I visit a bar, restaurant, hotel, museum, or park; watch a movie; or listen to a song a professional experience. I'm always working and observing, almost to a fault, but this is not a complaint. I'm looking at old and new concepts and their execution and service. It's inspiring and possible betterment for my businesses. Pro experience does not complete someone for a role; you have to keep getting better at your job, stay open to new or outside ideas, and consider compromise.

What are some job perks that you enjoy?

I have a schedule that is favorable to my family life, wife, and seven-year-old daughter. Most nights I can still see my daughter to sleep before I go to work.

I get to surround myself with a hand-chosen staff of people I respect and whose company I enjoy. We work together through thick and thin. Everything from my lawyer, handyman, auto mechanic, babysitter, accountant, dentist—you get the hint—are relationships cultivated through the hospitality industry.

What makes Debonair Social Club different from a typical nightclub?

Debonair is inspired by the elements of a typical mega nightclub but executed in a boutique environment. There are several bar stations, multiple levels, unique environments, two dance floors, booth seating, booming sound and video system, DJ and live music capabilities, and restroom attendants that add a touch of class. We just package and program it differently from a downtown or tourist venue. The name Debonair was an inside cheeky compliment to the hipsters and influencers we were trying to attract to our concept, and "social club" had a historical neighborhood appeal. Our branding has always had the moniker "Music, Food, Art, Romance, Dancing." The bar is a center city, an "anything can happen" nightclub.

How would you describe the Debonair Social Club crowd?

A music-driven inclusive mix. Originally, we were going after hipsters, artists, and cool kids. After thirteen years, we realized that even the original twenty-one- through twenty-five-year-olds are now in their thirties and going out a lot less. So ongoing, we try to reach younger people and always reach out to different music-driven audiences along the way.

A majority of our business is generated on weekends. Fridays and Saturdays are party people, including weekend warriors. These kids follow new music, trends, each others' socials, and of course sneakers. They are drawn to EDM (not a bad word) and huge music festivals, and they usually accompany their alcohol with some legal party favors (we do have a zero-tolerance drug policy).

The luxury of two floors is to create two separate environments. On the larger main floor, entertain the large parties, bottle service booths, bachelorettes and birthday celebrations, with high-energy, remixed top-forty, hip-hop, and newly released dance tracks. In the basement lounge, we can offer an avant-garde product and cater to a more fringe market. There, we experiment with younger or newer DJs and promoters that might not drive enough bodies for the main floor but still bring new faces and interesting formats, which are great or noteworthy for the venue and its exposure. It's a team effort that helps define the makeup of the Debonair audience.

Weekdays and specific events have an older draw: Drum and bass and house music (twenty-five- through thirty-five-year-olds). Fast-driving beat-hippies and house-heads.

Eighties New Wave draws people aged twenty-five through fifty-five: older clientele, eighties new wave fans, goth, synth, and punk fans. Some new, younger commuter and creative college types who like the old stuff. In Debonair's recent past, we hosted an eight-year-long production called the No-Tell Motel burlesque and cabaret every Wednesday. There were rotating troupes that created new productions.

What is different about Chicago nightlife culture versus other party destinations such as Las Vegas, Miami, Los Angeles, and New York City?

In my opinion, first, Chicago is not known for its glitz and celebrity appeal. Chicago is Midwest and not an entertainment or party tourist destination. The bars and neighborhoods are divided by locality, social economics, and cultural characteristics. The people who frequent certain areas based on music genre appeal to the peoples' culture and subcultures. Chicago locals are loyal and consider themselves to be regulars at their favorite haunts.

The nightclubs are affected negatively because of gentrification, whether it be rising rents or noise complaints. Same old story: nightlife finds desolate or sometimes emerging areas to garner affordable operating costs; the neighborhood becomes desirable by developers because of interest and cache; and rents, taxes, and new buildings rise, forcing out the younger or lower economic community. However, bigger-budget, more glamorous Downtown and River North nightclubs that are more tourist driven have a greater mix of suburbanites (bridge and tunnel crowd), similar to Miami, Las Vegas, and certain parts of New York City and LA.

Describe the general components of a nightlife marketing plan. What goes into promoting the nightclub experience, and how does Debonair Social Club constantly build buzz and evolve to stay relevant?

General components of nightlife marketing are composed of those textbook ideals, plus our individual spin offered to make it special and stand out from the pack. On opening Debonair, we secured effective press reach, sought out industry influencers, nurtured online presence (Facebook, Instagram, etc.), made service industry chatter, and aligned grassroots efforts in our neighborhood. We are lucky to be in an entertainment corridor.

The Debonair plan is to do something special once or more each quarter. These special-event bookings, or loss leaders, were to capture more attention than dollars. A DJ or band that usually plays for venues many times our size and capacity would leave a huge, favorable impression on the people who are important to our brand. These events sell out, and post press is at times more influential than the actual advertising that drove the event. This keeps Debonair current or sparkled in the nightlife community. We keep these bookings close to the brand but still pushing the envelope. Some examples of bookings both DJ and live band sets:

Steve Aoki (DJ, producer, electro house music)

Felix the Housecat (house music, dance, Chicago-born, international appeal)

Marky Ramone (punk legend, dance DJ set)

MIA (DJ set, rap and dance)

Thom Yorke, Radiohead (lead singer, DJ Set)

Bands (to name a few): Local H, Urge Overkill, MGMT, Alkaline Trio

Have there been measurable benefits from using social media? If so, what are they, and how have you measured them?

I believe there are measurable benefits. Facebook has detailed diametric analysis charting to show you the reach from your advertising dollars. It's unclear how accurate or effective these reports are. I personally think that we measure the benefits as positive by realizing the harm when events are not posted and boosted. Using social media, like any form of marketing, needs a full-court press. We try to have everyone who is involved in or who benefits from a successful event share on their personal and business pages. That means each bartender, security, manager, promoter, talent—all be aligned and sharing the same message promoting the event. We see a team effort in every aspect of the business. Social media is a layer and is as important as every other marketing layer.

Who are some of your mentors, and why are they quality leaders in your eyes?

My mentors in the nightlife industry are Cal Fortis (Big Time Design) and Ken Barilich. These Chicago guys owned and operated the Crobar Nightclubs locally and nationally. They also had several other venues under their umbrella. I was impressed by them because they were hands-on and grew the company adding cutting-edge concepts to their portfolio—everything from a bistro to punk-rock club, to sports bar and mega-nightclub. I worked for and with them for close to twenty years. I was honored with a sweat equity partnership in the early 2000s.

As far as I can remember, these gentlemen preached a game plan that is still viable these days: create and operate businesses that would be new to market, adhere to the story through design and build, operate and market on brand, hire with one hundred percent inclusion, be proactive, and put back into the business and the people who helped along the way.

How has working in the nightlife industry affected your own social life (sacrifices, trade-offs, access, etc.)?

I was fortunate enough to meet my wife and raise my family by means of the industry—can't say more than that. Socially, outside my immediate family, many friends have come and gone, accompanied with tons of laughs and tears alike.

For the next generation of twenty-one-year-olds, how would you show them the ropes to the nightlife industry?

Learn the basics and trust the building blocks of any good business. Don't skip or take lightly of the process. Great ideas are plenty, so make them credible by supporting them by creating a complete business plan. The exercise will flush out ideas and force you to answer the tough questions. You will gain confidence and will be able to sell the idea to raise investment if need be.

Surround yourself with a great team, and cast it like a movie or any pro team. Best players in the best positions. Everyone must be aligned in the vision and concept, with all on the same page to flow past any hurdles or indifferences. The common goal will rise above personal likes or personalities. Plus, everyone wants to be sharing the same concept to press and selling the same experience to clients walking in the door.

And of course, get a job in the business to learn by experience. You have to actually swing at a fastball to be able to hit the fastball—can't just read how to do it.

Devil May Care
Photographer: James Johnson

CHAPTER 7:
AUSTIN—JACK ZIMMERMANN AND MATTHEW NAPOLILLI

"Fake shots have become a thing for me."

Another city I was not too familiar with, but definitely wanted to include, is Austin, Texas. More people and businesses, especially in the technology industry, are moving to Austin than ever before because of the job opportunities, affordability, and overall quality of life. This rise in popularity is bound to have a positive impact on the city's nightlife scene. I was eager to interview Jack Zimmermann and Matthew Napolilli, who are two fascinating nightlife pros making their mark on this beloved southern city.

Beginning with Jack, he founded Nova Hospitality after working in the industry for several years as an avenue to explore both focused consulting and comprehensive management projects. He owns a moody lounge called Devil May Care and is close to opening an indoor-outdoor nightlife venue called Mayfair that sits above his chic restaurant TenTen; by design, Devil May Care, TenTen, and Mayfair are just feet from one another. I loved getting Jack's perspective on the business because he gave me great insight into what it's like to be a nightlife consultant rather than just an owner and operator. Jack has both local and international experience and has helped several nightlife venues become what they are today. Because Austin's nightlife scene is just beginning to expand, he is certainly one of the frontrunners in the industry there.

Jack's newest restaurant and lounge collaboration project is a prime example of why nightlife venues are often attached to a restaurant or hotel, because the hospitality businesses bounce off of each other well. Nightclubs and restaurants are a great way to bring traction to the hotel and get people to stay there and make vacations out of it. Tourists are also more drawn to hotels that have the perks of cool, popular restaurants and clubs. This symbiotic relationship adds to the guest experience.

I worked at High Rooftop, which is located on the roof of Hotel Erwin in Venice, California, one summer, and I witnessed that firsthand. Some groups of friends would get a hotel room to have the pregame or get faster access to the rooftop, and then they would go out to a different venue later in the night. Other examples of this set up include LIV inside the Fontainebleau in Miami, PHD Rooftop Lounges above the Dream Hotels in New York City, and The Bungalow at the Fairmont in Santa Monica.

Then there are some restaurants that turn into nightclubs during the later hours of the evening, or they are positioned near each other, like Jack's TenTen, Devil May Care, and Mayfair collaboration project. Either way, the combination of all the hospitality projects works and can definitely enhance the night-out experience. In Jack's case, guests can make an entire night out of visiting all three venues.

Furthermore, I appreciated that Jack expressed his in-depth strategy about making sure he hires DJs who can read the room and managers who make sure it's a positive experience for partygoers. Many clubs simply go through the motions and do not realize that every night has a different crowd and a different energy, so it really is important to have people managing the timing of the party and ensuring the energy flows. Similar to what Nick Montealegre and Frankie Delgado mentioned in the Los Angeles chapter, the quality of the DJs and their music playlists are key because that synergy is often one of the reasons why partygoers will be having the best night and not even realize why. It is because the music is seamlessly matching the energy level and the crowd's vibe.

Jack also introduces Steve Lieberman, the lighting expert he hired for his club, Mayfair. Steve's repertoire is very impressive: he's worked on Coachella, LIV in Miami, and the TAO properties in NYC. Nightclub lighting and special effects were also something I always noticed when going out because it was evident that the clubs that matched the music, lighting, and special effects were better at putting on the show. I was less impressed by the clubs that have random lasers going throughout the night.

When I interned at the nightclub Royale Boston, I sat in the technology booth some nights and watched how they programmed the lights, smoke machines, graphics on the screens, and more. These special effects emphasize the music playing and complement the vibe in the room. When the bass drops and the fire, smoke, and lights go crazy, the entire crowd's heart rate spikes up.

One of my favorite episodes of Netflix's *Abstract* was the one featuring London-based stage designer Esmeralda "Es" Devlin, who is renowned for her expertise in fusing music and lighting for large-scale productions. She has built the concert-tour stages for Beyoncé, Adele, U2, Kanye West, and many other artists. The episode relates to nightlife venues because they are smaller-scale productions, and they are similar to concerts in the sense that they also set a mood for an experience involving music and entertainment.

Another nightlife pro in Austin, Matthew Napolilli, has played an integral part in making Summit Austin one of the hottest nightclub destinations in the city. Matthew and the Summit team have successfully incorporated features of big-city nightclubs into Summit, such as bottle service and top-tier DJs, that are not as prevalent in Austin's nightlife scene. As Matthew mentions in his interview, Summit's location in Austin allows them to get a range of mid-tier to A-list artists. As Austin continues its economic expansion and growth as a hot travel destination, more and more A-list artists will perform.

Another part of Matthew's role is curating brand partnerships that help Summit stay relevant.

As seen on their social media, some of their nights include Bumble appearances. I think dating app partnerships make total sense because nightlife venues are places where people can meet, mingle, and maybe even find that special someone. With the plethora of brands out there, customized nightlife experiences can be an effective way to launch a new product or service, promote an existing product or service, and celebrate a company's successes and milestones. Strong brand partnerships are mutually beneficial and allow for both brands' networks to integrate. Working on these strategic partnerships is only one bullet point on Matthew's to-do list. Later in this chapter, Matthew gives us an inside look into not only a day-in-the-life but also a career-in-the-life of a nightlife professional.

Austin's nightlife scene seems to have always provided a good time, but with an increase in popularity for travel and living, I think their nightlife scene is about to boom. It is a prime place for nightlife because they have the ability to focus on the locals, students at the large universities, and tourists. With Jack's strong management skills, worldliness, eye for design, and quality service, he is undoubtedly going to upgrade Austin's nightlife scene.

Please enjoy learning more through my conversation with Jack.

Where are you originally from, and why did you choose for Nova Hospitality to be based in Austin?

I'm half English. I was born in London and grew up there as a kid. I went to high school in Dallas but did my first year of college back in London, and then I came across and finished university in Austin. I kind of bounced around a lot. I think because I had so many friends after finishing school, I just stayed in Austin, because it was at the time becoming one of the hottest cities for young people to live after school. I think I had such a network there that while I lived in Vegas, Austin was always my vacation. I would go probably twice a year to Austin just to catch up with people. It was always a place I gravitated back to.

So after I left Wynn, I did several years of consulting internationally, but always with the view of finding my way back to Austin to do my own ventures. It's also a smaller market, and at the time it was very much a B market. So to come in and do something with a smaller budget—nightlife, restaurants—for a couple of million bucks as opposed to the gigantic budgets you need to even compete in New York or Miami or Vegas, Austin was always appealing on that front too.

It's always been a fun scene in Austin, maybe not very refined. But, yeah, it's growing rapidly. The food and beverage and entertainment and hospitality scene as a whole is catching up now. So, yeah, it's a good time to be here.

How did you get started in the nightlife and hospitality industries?

At a bar back in Austin, Texas, when I was a sophomore in college. After several months, I decided to start hosting my own events and spent the rest of my college career putting on nightlife events for my college through a company that I named Afterdark Entertainment. It's still active today but now books DJs.

What made you want to work in nightlife and hospitality?

Initially, as a nineteen-year-old, it just seemed like a fun way to earn money. After transitioning to planning and hosting events, my passion for the industry started to develop. The thrill of conceptualizing and then executing, with all the minutiae in between, both grand and curated experiences, is what has driven me since. Watching the process from ideation to execution excites me beyond belief.

Describe your day-to-day and night-to-night responsibilities as founder and operator at Nova Hospitality.

What a mixed bag that is! I work every day, and each day is different. Let's triage this into three categories: businesses that are currently operating, projects that are currently in development, and future concepts.

For my businesses that are operating, I will play the facilitator role. Managers and directors report to me, and I will support them to ensure departments are operating as efficiently as possible and working well among one another. Further, I will attempt to be as present as possible during peak business hours, sometimes playing the role of host.

Projects that are in some stage of development will require a totally different use of time. Some of the main tasks here involve the raising of capital and investor relations, as well as concept development, design, budgeting, permitting, construction, and project management. As openings approach, the prelaunch marketing plans must take shape, as should the recruitment plans. Personally, I play a pivotal role in all these elements, directing the team to ensure we stay on-brand and within budget.

For future concepts, time is spent on diligence, an effort to gather as much information as possible to inform our decision—go or no-go—or the direction of our proposal. This category can take many shapes and forms. Sometimes a business is for sale, and we are considering making the purchase. Or perhaps there's a developer looking for a great tenant. For consultancies, RFPs (requests for proposals) come in, and we need to decide whether to bid on them or not. If we decide to, then we discuss how much time, effort, and money to put into said proposal, and which disciplines—operations, marketing, programming, accounting and finance, human resources, events, and the list goes on—to include.

On a day-to-day basis, I engage in current, upcoming, and future potential business activities. It keeps me on my toes!

What previous professional experiences have helped you most in this role?

After leaving Wynn Las Vegas, I spent the next sixteen months on four projects in four different countries. Each project had unique sets of problems and wildly different product offerings. It was an incredibly challenging time for me and a wonderful opportunity to grow.

Looking back at my experience, I was only getting started when I got hired at Wynn. It was my first job. I started in a true line-level position. I was a busser at XS and Tryst, after having owned my own modest company in Austin already. So I was going to try, and you're working at the very best, top places in the world. It was really exciting. I wouldn't actually say the culture there has a wonderful sort of team and ethos culture, but it's this culture of excellence that you don't really get in many other places. It's the best in the city that is probably the best in the world in what it does. And so you're kind of imbued with this air of excellence. And so at Wynn you really do learn how to do things very well from a customer service standpoint, cleanliness and thoroughness, and all that. Wynn was wonderful in ingraining those ideals in me.

There are some downsides, and it took me a few years after leaving Wynn to be really able to point them out, and maybe it's just being part of such a big machine that really makes creativity fall to the wayside. There's a lot more room to do much more interesting and exciting things there, but somewhere up the line, they just stop, and that's unfortunate because the place has big budgets and probably a lot more to offer than ever gets realized. It's why a lot of the top talent ends up leaving, and really interesting and creative folks move on from there to go off and do their own things, as opposed to sticking around and earning a good, solid paycheck that's offered there because you get bored. That's really why I left. I was so bored out of my mind.

Why did you decide to start a hospitality group that focuses on consulting, management, and partnerships for restaurants and nightclubs? What hospitality management tips do you think restaurants and nightclubs need the most today?

Beyond the fact that hospitality and F&B (food and beverage) are my main areas of competency, I saw an avenue that would help me gain access to lots of great projects. Instead of simply being a proprietor, owning a couple of my own ventures, Nova allows me to engage with numerous potential projects and to market ourselves to the outside world. Also, there is a real need for expert help in this industry.

Tip: Do not proceed without experienced and talented folks on your team. Find those people, compensate them well, and treat them better. Many places open their doors through an idea and some financial backing, and then things quickly go awry or nestle into the realm of mediocrity. What's typically missing from these projects is the talented people who can take them to the heights they had imagined.

What are some of the biggest challenges of opening a nightlife venue?

For starters, the various design aspects. Without a food or craft cocktail offering to differentiate you, a USP (unique selling point), the various design elements are your main products on offer: branding, architectural, interior, and lighting. With a blank canvas, there are so many options, and the aforementioned disciplines must work well together. Then, sourcing the numerous operating supplies, vendors, equipment, finishes, and fixtures is a whole different beast.

Brand positioning and concept definition can be tricky components too. Who are we, and who is our target audience? Okay, now how do we reach them?

Lastly, as an opening approach, there is a chaotic, several-week phase comprised of recruitment, on-boarding, training, soft opening, and launch. Picking the right staff, training them well, and leading them effectively will inform the degree of early success an operation has.

What are Nova Hospitality's current projects? What makes them different from typical hospitality properties in Austin?

I'm the operating partner of a private membership club on the east side of town. East Austin is sort of the emerging side of town. Downtown has been the central hub for a long time, but the east side has really come a long way from the food, beverage, and nightlife scene. So I've got a private members' club on the east side that's called Pershing. There's a Soho House opening in Austin, and really, those two will always be compared to one another. Although they are quite different, the price point and membership is about the same. I didn't open Pershing, but the equity owner reached out to me last year, and my group Nova now oversees the business on his behalf.

TenTen and Mayfair are two businesses in the same building, so they're dead smack in the middle of downtown. That's 501 West Sixth, about as good a location as you can get in terms of bulkability for high-rise residential, offices, and hotels.

So those two businesses in there are my babies, and then the building as a whole, there are two other sorts of entertainment-centric businesses in there, and Nova will oversee some components for them. I don't own those businesses, but we'll do a management agreement, and Nova will take on some of the infrastructure stuff that they don't want to have to go out and worry about. I've also taken over a place at 500 West Sixth, so right across the street, and it's a restaurant that turns into a cocktail lounge with a strong event component.

With TenTen, we are building a total-package restaurant. Many restaurants in Austin have great food, and others have a nice ambiance or a strong beverage program. Few have great service, and almost none have all the above. We have put immense effort into our food, design, and beverage offerings. Our service will be of the highest level, and the vibe will be fantastic.

With Mayfair, nothing like it exists in Austin at the moment. It was very important to me that we had an indoor and outdoor component and that the lounge could transform throughout the night from a classy, sexy, cozy lounge to a high-energy, Vegas-style nightclub. Our music will be highly curated, and we will have the absolute best service Austin has ever seen. The lighting design we have implemented will also be extraordinary, and it's Steve Lieberman's first project in Texas.

Steve Lieberman is a guru in nightlife and festival lighting. Coachella and Electric Daisy Carnival are two of his big clients. He designs the main stage and how that's going to look, with all the LED walls, and all the lights, and all the really creative use of the newest technology. He's got a finger on the pulse of what's new in the lighting world—brand-new lasers and fog machines and all the different components. He brings them all together. Festivals are really his baby, but nightclubs he could accept. He did LIV. He's done most of the clubs in LA and San Diego because LA's home for him. He does the TAO Group properties in New York, including Marquee. He's just an absolute legend in nightlife lighting and all that.

What is the relationship between Nova Hospitality and your clients?

It's with a management company where as many facets of a business as necessary can be tapped on to us, and my group can basically take a lot of the difficult things off of an owner's plate.

A lot of smaller businesses can't really afford a director, a finance and accounting team, and social media manager, and they kind of do their best. What will often happen is that there's a GM (general manager) of a nightclub, and I can speak for here in Austin, but a GM of a nightclub might be paid close to say six figures. That person is tasked with overseeing the staff and the customer experience, and making sure the right amount of liquor is ordered for a weekend, and all the other hundreds of normal operating responsibilities. But then on top of that, they're in charge of hiring, training, and firing, which are tedious and processes that often have a legal component. On top of that, there are social media accounts that should be managed in the office and that don't get any love, let alone bookkeeping, accounting, finance, and any number of other tasks, like photo, video graphic design. It often ends up falling on the plate of one GM, who is filling a lot of their gaps and getting totally burned out because now they're working seventy-five, eighty hours a week just to get it all done, and none of it is getting done very well. By engaging with a company like Nova, you can pass off all that stuff to pros, and you can build at a much lower hourly rate than if you're going to an independent third party for all of them.

What is different about Austin nightlife culture versus other party destinations, such as Miami, Los Angeles, Las Vegas, and New York City?

Austin has a great bar scene. For a smaller city, the sheer number of beverage establishments is impressive. There is wonderful weather in Austin too, so the daytime party scene is stronger than anywhere I can recall. What's different? Well, Austin is a very casual city compared to the markets mentioned. People don't get dressed up as much, and the establishments and their pricing match the lower-key approach.

It's not a very developed scene here. It's not very competitive on the Vegas-style nightclub side of things. There are hundreds of bars in Austin, so there's a big nightlife scene, but just not the nightclub scene. So really, what we do is going to dictate what's to follow.

Describe the general components of a nightlife marketing plan. What goes into promoting the nightclub experience, and how do nightclubs constantly build buzz and evolve to stay relevant?

In this day and age, digital content is primary, and I don't mean flyers. Real, high-quality photo, video, and graphic design with imagery that speaks to your desired audience. Tell a story and avoid flyers, even digital ones, as much as possible. Grassroots marketing can be a great asset too, if you have the right team. Incentivizing the staff to promote through their social circles and their social media accounts can add a level of cool factor. Within grassroots marketing, developing relationships with hotel concierges and other influential locals can be of value. Lastly, throw great events. Nothing markets a venue better than an exciting themed party or top-tier musical act, so be creative in your programming and then put out great content to let the world know about it or to show folks what they may have missed.

Staying relevant can be challenging. Improving your physical space, upgrading lighting and sound, ongoing team training, fine-tuning customer service, CRM (customer relationship management), and taking risks on talent programming—all require capital and effort.

Many clubs open their doors, but few redefine themselves or remain vigilant to shifting trends. It's key for longevity.

Have there been measurable benefits from using social media? If so, what are they, and how have you measured them?

I don't have examples of hard metrics for success with social media, but I'd say that the benefits are immeasurable. Marketing campaigns take time to show up on click counts, revenue reports, or P&Ls (profit and loss statements), but there is no doubt that the good ones work. That said, when forty people post a well-crafted teaser video at the same time and flood social media channels, there is an immediate public response in the form of web traffic, inquiries, and reservations.

Is Austin very promoter-driven?

I don't like working with promoters at all. I wouldn't mind working with a promoter if they were going to do their own nights with us. So an off-night, like a Sunday or Thursday, if they had an interesting concept that was still a fit for our brand. It can't be some eighteen-and-up hip-hop party. It needs to be a brand fit. If it is, then we could work with their promoter to do their own night, so our guests know it's not a normal Mayfair night, it's this other thing. For the most part, that's the extent I'll do with a promoter. It just gets to be a sleazy thing. You lose control in your own venue if you sell your soul. That's big in Miami and LA. None of that in Austin.

We will hire our own internal team who should be qualified to help promote the venue. And then, like I mentioned, we're not just going to create flyers, which are incredibly boring and painful to even look at. We actually have our creative department put together great photo imagery and videos with music overlays and a little bit of graphic design, and we actually come get photos of the staff as the nights are getting going, in their uniforms, and as the night's beginning. And then creating a small database of content for our staff to choose from to post on their own so we're not just sort of mandating social media campaigns for our staff. Basically, we give them the option and the right to do so, but we do not force it down their throats because a cocktail waitress signed up to be a cocktail waitress, not have to post three times a week.

What does the hiring process for a nightclub look like? How does your Human Resources professional, Connie Ballew, decide who will make the nightclub operate successfully? How is performance managed for nightlife roles, such as bartenders, bottle service girls, DJs, bouncers, and others?

With nightlife recruitment, we handpick management personnel and employ them around a month from opening. They'll get started on numerous pre-opening items and will work with HR on the recruitment strategy. In nightlife, it's most effective to create an exciting video or graphic, sharing the details of an upcoming casting call. The hope is that hundreds of folks show up for a limited number of jobs. We evaluate experience, attitude, and aptitude. For me, upbeat and positive attitudes matter above all else. The role of a top HR person like Connie is more that of a facilitator in these scenarios, as opposed to final decision-maker on hire or pass. She should make sure the process is smooth and well organized and that the candidates receive hire or pass communication in a timely manner. Then she will begin on-boarding folks and working with operations management to get them the necessary training material and schedule. Finally, Connie is a guardian of our team culture and should constantly reinforce our values.

Performance management for all positions is integral to long-term success. Set standards, communicate them clearly, answer any questions, observe performance, coach in the moment, follow up with direct feedback, check for understanding, and then remain vigilant for pattern behavior. It's important to communicate clearly and maintain patience throughout the process, but you must also know when to make a difficult decision. All positions receive the same treatment, just with different measures of performance.

What do you think is the best layout and vibe for a nightclub, bar, and lounge? What are key components to designing each? How did you and your interior designer, Lisa Escobar, decide Mayfair's layout and vibe?

Indoor-outdoor, with a variety of experiential options in one venue. Not everyone wants the same experience. The flow of the room is of the utmost importance. These rooms can get very busy, and the way people are able to flow is key. Beyond that, there should be focal points and eye-catching details in the lighting and finishes.

Layout for Mayfair was informed by our overall space. We wanted two-thirds lounge and one-third terrace. We also wanted to pick a timeless, historical theme as opposed to modern and edgy, which will become dated over time. By choosing a Victorian theme, we were able to have some fun in using old-world finishes in a modern nightlife environment. A good example is our mirror-finished LED screens, which will be set within Victorian picture frames. When the screens are off, they'll look like late-1800s mirrors; when they're on, they will run video content. Lisa is really talented, and our final product will be pretty special.

What is your strategy for nightclub programming?

Our strategy on the programming side, if we're talking about DJs, is really tiers one, two, and three. Tier one would be the A-list celebrity DJs. We don't want to book too many tier-one DJs in year one because what happens—and I have been part of this and watched this—is a lot of these clubs get in a habit of booking them, and basically it ends up being a loss leading exercise. So you spend seventy-five thousand dollars on a DJ, and you don't make all your money back. However, there's a lot of cool factor, and there's a line around the block trying to get in for that DJ. The club says, "Yeah, we lost money, but it was such great marketing." And then they do it again the next month because nobody wants to show up to the club unless they've got that DJ again, or another great DJ, and so it turns into a downward spiral. We don't want to do that. For tier-one DJs, we will pay the high expense when we can make the money back or if we get what we perceive as good value on a DJ. So if a tier-one DJ usually costs one hundred fifty thousand dollars, but because they're in Texas already you can get them for seventy-five thousand dollars, that might be the time we'd pull the trigger. Or if it's a very big weekend in Austin in which a lot of tourists are in town, that might be a good time to pull the trigger on a tier-one DJ. So basically, anywhere from five to eight per year of the celebrity DJs or artists.

The tier-two people are the recognizable DJs from the A market. The clubs have five or six good DJs and a lot of people know their names. Las Vegas, New York, Miami, and LA all have a few of these DJs. They're only about two to three thousand dollars, including their flight and hotel. It's not something you want to do every night because some people don't know their names, but it's something you keep in mind because then in a couple of months, you might be like, "All right. These guys actually play great music, and they're only a couple of grand." And there are a lot of people who recognize their name from the one time they went to XS in Vegas, TAO in New York, LIV in Miami, etc. Tier three is just the local guys.

We're going to heavily curate as well. DJs are going to have to audition just like a cocktail waitress or bartender might. There's a process. We don't just hire the DJs whom everybody knows around town. We're actually looking for people who can read a room and make changes on the fly, and they don't just come in and play whatever they decided they were going to play the night before.

There's room for everything. There's room for pop these days, and definitely hip-hop. EDM is sort of tapering off a little bit, but definitely some of that. Latin music is pretty popular these days. We really just want DJs who can play a great set and hopefully touch lots of bases.

What are some job perks in the nightlife industry that you enjoy?

Invitations to events of all kinds. There is a little bit of local fame that comes with being an operator of a top nightclub.

Who are some of your mentors, and why are they quality leaders in your eyes?

In all honesty, I am yet to have a mentor within this industry. There are some folks whose work I admire, but that's where it ends. My mentors include Tony Hsieh for his work in culture formation and creating wonderful places to work, and Brene Brown for her writing on personal development; I've been able to apply much of her writing to my work. There are some groups that have very high-level F&B concepts that I admire. Inception group is one that takes a creative approach to this industry, and I appreciate their attention to detail.

Leadership qualities I admire include the willingness to give autonomy to team members, equanimity, and the ability to praise the team for victories and assume responsibility for losses.

How has working in the nightlife industry affected your own social life (sacrifices, trade-offs, access, etc.)?

In my Vegas, Miami, and Dubai days, I worked all night long and slept until midafternoon. It was hard on the body and overall wellness. It's suboptimal from a relationship standpoint too. These days, my schedule is much healthier. There is, however, an expectation to play host and be present, and everyone wants to buy the owner a drink. Fake shots have become a thing for me.

For the next generation of twenty-one-year-olds, how would you show them the ropes to the nightlife industry?

I'd encourage them to start in a line-level position, master it, and then work their way up. All the while, they should be as observant as possible while out for food and drinks or other experiences, identifying likes and dislikes, writing them down and considering how each venue they visit could be better. Be a sponge, ask questions, read books, and soak it all up. There are no shortcuts here.

Where do you see Nova Hospitality in the next five years?

In five years, Nova will own and/or operate more than ten high-level F&B and nightlife establishments across a handful of top markets. We'll continue to build our senior team—some of the best folks in their respective fields, who live and breathe our ethos—to facilitate such rapid growth.

Summit

"Ultimate organized chaos!"

Please enjoy learning more through my conversation with Matthew.

How did you get started in the nightlife and hospitality industries?

I have basically been in the industry my entire life, working in kitchens and bussing tables. However, it got serious when I moved to Las Vegas in 2000 to attend University of Nevada, Las Vegas. I worked on opening eight of the biggest clubs in the world.

What made you want to work in nightlife?

I was attending the hotel and beverage administration program at University of Nevada, Las Vegas when I applied for a job at ICE nightclub that changed my life forever. From ICE I moved to Pure nightclub in Caesars Palace, and from Pure to Wet Republic and director of VIP marketing of the MGM Grand. Then to Light Group, opening Haze, LIQUID Pool Lounge, Gold Ultra Lounge, then to open Marquee and Marquee day club at the Cosmopolitan.

Describe you day-to-day and night-to-night responsibilities at Summit. What is your official title?

Director of operations and marketing. Monday through Thursday, 10:00 a.m. to 4:30 p.m., office hours—programming music as fit for the night and time of year, private parties, one-offs, etc. Social media management. Hiring process and recruitment. Liquor sponsorships and partnerships. Overseeing overall maintenance and wear-and-tear of property.

Thursday through Saturday, 8:00 p.m. to 2:30 a.m.—operating hours, production.

What previous professional experiences have helped you most in this role?

Being a people person is very important, and communication is key in sales. However, being present and training in each position is vital so you can respect all job duties and understand what they entail.

What makes Summit different from a typical nightclub?

Summit is what we call "Ultimate organized chaos!" It looks like the wheels will fall off at any given moment, however it's a well-oiled machine. The layout of the night club makes it supper intimate, ultra-private, and safe all at the same time.

Nightlife experiences on rooftops have become extremely popular. How has having a rooftop deck benefitted Summit's business?

The view is amazing, and you have to see because pictures don't do it justice. Some of the best parties we have had in the past are when it rains, to be honest. People lose all inhibitions and go nuts and start spraying champagne. It's something you have to experience firsthand.

What is different about Austin nightlife culture versus other party destinations, such as Las Vegas, Miami, Los Angeles, and New York City?

Austin is in its infancy still, it's still the Wild West here, and yes, cops ride horses here! What makes this city special is that we are not tainted like the bigger cities, and we still get to write our own story here. A lot of the big talent agencies almost treat us like a third-world country down here with pricing, which we are more than happy with because it allows us to get some big-name performers down here and still be able to make a profit on the shows. We are able to be laid-back while being professional at the same time and deliver an experience like no other.

Describe the general components of a nightlife marketing plan. What goes into promoting the nightclub experience, and how does Summit constantly build buzz and evolve to stay relevant?

That's the thing—to stay relevant! "Out of sight, out of mind" social media with staff is vital! Using your staff's reach helps the company brand go further and be repetitive. Effective programming and studying trends is important as well. Knowing what's hot and changing it up—don't get stuck with the same stuff all the time, take chances. Sure, you might fail, but at least you tried.

Have there been measurable benefits from using social media? If so, what are they, and how have you measured them?

Yes, major! It is possible to boost your postings to accounts and extend a reach that was not there prior. Also, there are measurements to see how successful your campaigns are and to see how to improve moving forward. This also helps capture data for the venue as well, which makes every attempt that much easier.

How does Summit choose its promoters? What is their role?

Typically they choose us. In this industry, you get what you put in. If we are approached by a person or group, we do a test-drive; it's kind of the sink-or-swim method. We normally do this on an off night on which we do not operate. If they can show us they are capable of filling a room on a non-operating night, this shows us they know what they are doing.

Who are some of your mentors, and why are they quality leaders in your eyes?

I lived in Vegas for eighteen years, so I was brought up by some of the biggest guys in the business. Shawn Chester, VP of VIP services for Wynn and Light group, taught me to be more polished and professional and to grind harder. Alex Cordova taught me from a young age the importance of office hours and polishing up and managing my database.

How has working in the nightlife industry affected your own social life (sacrifices, trade-offs, access, etc.)?

You can start by saying goodbye to your weekends and holidays. For twelve years of my life, my day started at 3:00 p.m.—wake up, gym, eat, tan (working nights, you don't see much sun), then work, get off at 7:00 or 8:00 a.m., go eat, bed at 9:00 a.m., repeat.

What are some job perks that you enjoy?

Taking care of VIPs. There are many perks: the jets, best seats at concerts, sporting events, eating the best meals, golf. The perks are endless. However, getting caught up in the lifestyle can be bad as well.

For the next generation of twenty-one-year-olds, how would you show them the ropes to the nightlife industry?

Be humble and learn to crawl before you walk. Don't think you know it all, because you don't. Every day is a new experience to learn!

Summit

Tongue & Groove

CHAPTER 8

ATLANTA—MICHAEL KROHNGOLD

"Someone turns twenty-one every day, and they are the future."

One of my first nightclub experiences was when I visited my sister at Emory University, and she and her friends took me to Tongue & Groove in Buckhead, Atlanta. I have always been obsessed with celebrities, so they knew to describe the club as "Usher goes all the time!" I was pumped to say the least.

Atlanta is known for its music industry influence because a wide array of artists reside, produce music, and party in the city. I was excited at the mere thought of mingling and partying with some of the biggest names in entertainment. It is fitting that I went with an Emory crew, because the owners of Tongue & Groove are Atlanta locals and went to Georgia Tech and Emory. The club was noticeably respectful and inclusive, treating the Emory kids in their early twenties the same as the older and potentially wealthier customers. Starting customer loyalty early reaps benefits. Many graduates of these schools end up working in Atlanta or have friends who will. Speaking of inclusive, they even invited everyone who has ever been a customer to their twenty-fifth anniversary party. So nice and smart!

Michael Krohngold is one of the masterminds behind the club, along with Scott Strumlauf and current operating partner David Kreidler. Michael and Scott opened Tongue & Groove in 1994, and it has been an Atlanta staple ever since. When first learning about Michael and Scott's partnership, I found myself quickly drawing a comparison to that of Studio 54's dynamic duo, Ian Schrager and Steve Rubell. This connection was confirmed when Michael mentioned in his interview that Ian Schrager is in fact someone he admires. Krohngold handles the aesthetic and creative aspects of Tongue & Groove, and Strumlauf manages the financial and legal elements.

I love watching Tongue & Groove evolve yet keep the same general vibe. One way the venue has remained the same is in keeping the original name, which is a nod to the wood flooring used on a dance floor. On the other hand, the venue continues to grow and maintain relevance through their brand partnerships with other nightclubs around the country. For instance, the international TAO Group brought their nightclub team and party from all over to celebrate the Super Bowl at Tongue & Groove in 2019. This is simple co-promotion that benefits both nightlife brands.

Like other iconic nightclubs, Tongue & Groove is an incubator for emerging lifestyle trends in music, fashion, and art. Before social media, the real influencers were debuting such trends at the nightclubs. Tongue & Groove influences in both manners—digitally and in person. The success of the club says a great deal about Michael, Scott, and David's leadership. Every business has their fair share of issues, but the longevity of the club proves Tongue & Groove's superior management and customer service. Their commitment to the balance of business and party is evident. The loyalty is there and they are still bringing in new customers as the older crowd retires from the dance floor and the rising twenty-one-year-olds are entering the club week after week.

Similar to the other people featured in this book, Michael was interested in the industry at an early age. In the beginning stages of his career, he frequently went out to nightclubs and saw the lucrative opportunities in the industry and ran with it. He met many people along the way in every role—bartenders, bouncers, lighting technicians, and more—whom he could then bring to his own venue eventually. Now the club has been operating for twenty-six years. What says good management better than that? Tongue & Groove truly deserves to be Atlanta's longest-running nightclub.

Please enjoy learning more through my conversation with Michael.

How did you get started in the nightlife industry?

While a sophomore at Georgia Tech, I was hired as a doorman at Scooter's Neon Cowboy. I worked as a barback and eventually became a bartender.

What made you want to work in nightlife?

I enjoy music, art, design, and technology. The nightlife industry provided an opportunity to immerse myself in those disciplines.

Describe your day-to-day and night-to-night responsibilities at Tongue & Groove.

When we opened in 1994, I was a young(er) man. In 2008, my longtime business partner Scott Strumlauf and I offered our then much younger manager David Kreidler an opportunity to buy in as an operating partner. A few years later, we hired our current general manager, Jayne Branum. She has helmed the ship for quite some time and is extremely adept in all aspects of the business. This has enabled me to back off substantially from the daytime and nighttime operations. For years I had spearheaded front-of-the-house operations focusing on promotions, marketing, formatting, and the look and feel of the place. I enjoyed going in to see the place at full throttle and to observe the staff and patrons interactions. Hanging out at closing always provided keen insights.

A few years ago, I curtailed my daily and nightly hands-on responsibilities and delegated and trusted others. I now communicate daily and receive nightly logs that recap the previous night's business. We have weekly owner-manager meetings to discuss the previous week and upcoming events. We are currently planning a makeover of the club to coincide with our twenty-fifth anniversary in November of this year, which I half-jokingly refer to as my coming out of semiretirement.

What previous professional experiences have helped you most in this role?

I worked at other nightclubs in the Atlanta market—bartending at Confetti, managing at Club Rio—providing hands-on experience. I also worked at a boutique advertising and marketing agency after graduating college.

What makes Tongue & Groove different from a typical nightclub?

We truly foster a team mentality and strive to be nice to everyone: staff, customers, suppliers. We offer the comfort and familiarity of a neighborhood bar but the thrill and experience of a full-blown dance club.

What is different about Atlanta nightlife culture versus other party destinations, such as Las Vegas, Miami, Los Angeles, and New York City?

Southern hospitality truly exists, but try as we might, Atlanta is a second-tier city. Lesser cover charge and drink and bottle prices reflect the lower cost of living here. This in turn helps perpetuate our continued local following. The growth of the film industry has helped bring attention to the city, and the sports and music scene continue to give sizzle to the nightly crowds, but the market as a whole isn't as large as other top-tier cities.

Describe the general components of a nightlife marketing plan. What goes into promoting the nightclub experience, and how does Tongue & Groove constantly build buzz and evolve to stay relevant?

Nightly themes, musical formats, holiday tie-ins, special events, targeted markets, public relations, in-house graphic design, street promoters, and the notion of giving the best possible customer experience night after night to foster an environment of repeat business.

As music, fashion, and pop culture evolve, we strive to change and adapt accordingly. We reinvent regularly to keep the physical facility fresh, well maintained, and looking good.

Have there been measurable benefits from using social media? If so, what are they, and how have you measured them?

Of course, as evidenced by our continued success! It's pretty much our only outreach in terms of advertising and an immediate connection to our clientele. Followers, likes, and reposts serve partially as a barometer, but it's difficult to truly measure. Only when things go truly viral, or the nightly operations surge in terms of the number of patrons through the door and the energy of the night exceeds previous levels, can we begin to correlate our efforts to measurable benefits.

Who are some of your mentors, and why are they quality leaders in your eyes?

My father, Malcolm, who was a small businessman, taught me to stay grounded, humble, and focused. Ian Schrager, who remained behind the scenes for his years at Studio 54 with his keen design sense, trend-spotting, and attention to details. Eric Goode of Area fame [NYC nightclub] for his creativity in recreating the club every few months. He surrounded himself with the most artistic minds around. I didn't know either of these industry leaders personally; I simply followed their careers as inspiration.

How has working in the nightlife industry affected your own social life (sacrifices, trade-offs, access, etc.)?

Working in nightlife is oftentimes one's own social life. It has provided flexibility with hours worked. Working holidays such as the ultimate amateur night, New Year's Eve, is sometimes a blessing, while providing time off when others are at work. I was able to spend time with my son when he was young.

What are some job perks that you enjoy?

People are drawn by the smoke and mirrors and glitz and glamour associated with nightclubs. Working at a nightclub can provide a certain cache. If you're a regular, knowing someone at the front door and having a bartender who knows your name can give you the feeling that people want by belonging to a club. That of course grows exponentially with being an owner. People look to be your friend and often barter in some ways to reciprocate for VIP treatment. Liquor distributors often offer tickets to sporting events and suites for concerts. Reservations at hot restaurants are typically easier. Being recognized is a blessing and a curse.

For the next generation of twenty-one-year-olds, how would you show them the ropes to the nightlife industry?

Start at the bottom, work hard, and stay humble. Don't get sucked into the sometimes perils and temptations of the industry. Someone turns twenty-one every day, and they are the future. I look to the next generation for fresh ideas and what drives them. How do they want to spend their free time? An open exchange of ideas and sharing of information is helpful to all.

CHAPTER 9

MIAMI—JASON ODIO

"Social media is almost like people's report cards."

Like I said in the introduction, Miami is where I got my initial exposure to the nightlife industry, so naturally the city and its nightlife scene hold a special place in my heart. Miami is where I learned it all, from what to wear to how to get into a nightclub to how the overall night would typically flow in the club. I witnessed nightlife attire with girls in tight bandage dresses and sky-high heels, the way girls would flirt with the bouncers, how VIPs were putting on their own show beside the DJ booth, and how promoters were giving out their numbers to a bunch of girls and inviting them to drink for free at their table.

A lot of life is luck, and I was lucky enough to work at a place like World Red Eye, a multimedia agency in Miami, where everyone genuinely wanted to help me grow and learn. Not only did my boss, Seth Browarnik, take extra steps to teach me about the industry, but every single coworker was my mentor. Regardless of being a few years younger and less experienced, they all took me under their wing and greatly influenced my career path today. I will be forever grateful for them and that experience, and I am still very close to and look up to them. You know who you are. Thank you.

While working at World Red Eye, a Q&A with Jason Odio was one of the first assignments I worked on. I basically fixed one or two grammatical mistakes, but nonetheless I felt very involved and invested due to who the subject of the Q&A was. Jason's thoughts about his venues and the industry radiated off the page for me. Jason runs Native Sons Hospitality, which currently runs restaurants Baby Jane and Ariete and used to operate Sidebar, a beloved neighborhood party spot in Brickell, Miami.

Although Jason is mainly a restaurateur these days, after closing Sidebar in 2018, he has made quite an impact on the nightlife scene in the 305. With Sidebar, he filled a void for partygoers who didn't desire a megaclub, and he created a cool indoor-outdoor space where everyone felt comfortable partying. Jason's Q&A on WorldRedEye.com has always stuck with me because it was one of the first interviews I had read about someone in the hospitality and nightlife businesses. Yes, I greatly admire other Miami hotspots, such as LIV, Story, E11EVEN, and the other hundreds of places in the nightlife destination list, but Jason's approach to appeal to the

Miami locals as well as tourists from all areas, not just Miami Beach, always stood out to me. He effortlessly embraces Miami's art and music culture while providing venues that people have a good time at. He is a very smart and driven guy, and I have loved watching how he makes moves and affects the Miami hospitality and nightlife culture. I believe he mastered the balance of focusing on food and beverage, and music and programming, while not having a reputation of being overly exclusive and celebrity driven. His restaurants and bars are cool while having a more chill and inclusive vibe. When this interview was initially conducted, Jason was running his new concept in the Sidebar location called Kindred, which is currently La Otra Disco Bar.

In my follow-up call with Jason about a year later, I had the opportunity to get Jason's updated situation as the original Sidebar space went through various rebrands. We frankly discussed the successes and failures of the endeavor and how the current nightlife culture affected the direction of his venue.

Jason was kind of forced into rebranding Sidebar because the venue got shut down by the city after several issues. Sidebar had an open-door policy because it had an anti-nightclub and anti–South Beach policy, but it was hard to control the masses once Sidebar grew in popularity.

Sidebar prided itself on having a cool crowd where like-minded people could hang out, but that crowd eventually evolved into a younger crowd, and the older people did not necessarily want to associate with them. Regarding nightlife crowds, Jason mentioned how you cannot start with a bad crowd and work your way up to a better crowd. You always have to shoot for the best crowd, hope you get it, and try to maintain that as long as possible because what is considered the cool crowd is the first people to move on to the next best thing because they have access to multiple places, and every place is trying to pool from the same pot of cool people and trendsetters or people who are in the know. You try to maintain the best quality crowd as long as you can.

Once Sidebar's crowd started getting out of control and unmanageable, Jason and his team tried to implement new policies at the door, but it was almost too late at that point. The group of people turned into a not-so-desirable crowd. Business was still doing well, and they had good programming, but business dropped once they got shut down. Jason was not expecting the hiatus between the closing and reopening to affect the momentum of the space as much as it did.

While Sidebar was shut down, Jason and his team thought they would take the time to rebrand the space with a new name, Kindred, and a new vibe to lure in the original crowd. However, they were overly confident, and what they executed was not necessarily up to par with what the competition was doing. The competition grew immensely during the four and a half years that Sidebar was open. People were not fooled by the simple Kindred rebrand, and Jason feels that they did not do a good job delivering something fresh enough to get back their original cool crowd. Jason and the Kindred partners were not seeing eye to eye on the direction of the space, and fortunately they were able to shut down Kindred before it did too much harm to the venue.

The failure of Kindred was an eye-opener for Jason and his team because they did have a long run with Sidebar and major success with the space. He said it was humbling investing all this time and money into reinventing the space and then falling short. Next, Jason brought in new partners for the second rebrand, called Insideout, but that concept was also lacking in some areas. Finally, Jason was introduced to Marcelo Medina, who was prominent in the Latin community and did a great deal of nightlife programming. After exploring different opportunities, Jason ended up pitching Marcelo on the idea of transforming the space to fit Marcelo's Latin demographic, where he could be in charge of programming, promoters, and other parts of operations.

Insideout was just hanging on when it was open, and now La Otra, Jason and Marcelo's latest rebrand, is incredibly successful. Jason and Marcelo's partnership and concept worked because Latin music is thriving right now, especially in Miami. Latin music's popularity has become a fruitful formula for success in nightlife today. The Latin music scene was always something that Jason wanted to tap into, and Marcelo was his in to reach that demographic.

Another aspect of the nightlife industry that has changed over the years is the bottle service scene. Jason acknowledged that most people are not fooled and aren't as willing to spend the same on bottles and tables as they were in the past. However, he said that the Latin American partygoers in Miami are still excited by the bottle service experience and see the value in having the comfort of a table, so the bottle service scene is somewhat alive.

Overall, Jason went through plenty of ups and downs with the Sidebar location, and it is rewarding to see it come back to life as La Otra with a different crowd, music, look, and feel. It is also exciting that people are experiencing it for the first time because most of the young people had never been to Sidebar. Jason is certainly a fighter, and I admire him for his perseverance because he could have simply closed Sidebar's door and walked away. He surrounded himself with the right people and was not afraid to go back to the drawing board when a concept failed. Jason even entered the café and fast casual market by opening Bebito's while dealing with all these challenges.

Bebito's Casa de Cafecito is a Cuban coffee shop in Miami Beach. The aesthetics of his properties are always on point with quality food and beverages, friendly service, and some sort of artsy, Instagram-worthy décor. Bebito's is no different. Although Jason is currently transitioning from nightlife and focusing on this fast casual concept, I hope he considers using his nightlife expertise for a new bar or nightclub in the future. As for now, Jason's liquid courage will be coffee instead of vodka cranberries. I am excited to keep up with Jason's upcoming projects while enjoying the dining experiences at his current restaurants each time I come back to Miami.

His venues certainly stand out from the Miami clutter, and I love that he uses World Red Eye's platform to his advantage like most of the other restaurants and venues in Miami. Check out his restaurant concepts, as well as other Miami hotspots on WorldRedEye.com, and you will see why it is worth every hospitality and nightlife group's marketing dollars. The photographers do a great job at showcasing venues in an authentic way, catching real moments of real people in these unique venues.

Please enjoy learning more through my conversation with Jason.

How did you get started in the nightlife and restaurant industries?

I started when I was sixteen years old. A very close family friend, like a Cuban cousin, Roman Jones, let me do a high school night during the summer at one of his clubs. The night was very successful, and I think he saw the potential in me. When I was eighteen, I started working for him full time.

Describe your day-to-day and night-to-night responsibilities at Native Sons Hospitality.

No two days are alike. I try to balance spending time in the office and more importantly, onsite. I'm fortunate that at the moment, the three concepts that I own are all busy at different times. It allows me to do the rounds. I continue to try to structure my week a certain way, but with all the variables that come with this business, it's a bit hard.

How do La Otra, Baby Jane, and Ariete differentiate from one another, and what inspired the vibes and designs of each?

They're all very different. La Otra is a club and bar hybrid. Ariete is a casual fine-dining restaurant. Baby Jane is a cocktail bar and restaurant. I wanted to figure out where there was a void I could fill in each area. From there, I pictured what my friends and I would enjoy. As I get older and Miami keeps changing, there's a lot of opportunity to create a great and unique environment.

What is the biggest challenge of running three unique hotspots?

I would say managing expectations. You really have to know how to navigate a lot of different people, from your staff to guests and vendors. It's also a very competitive industry, so always trying to keep things fresh can be a challenge.

What are some job perks that you enjoy?

Free drinks! Just kidding. Even though it's very demanding, I'm thankful that I'm not stuck in a cubicle eight hours a day. It's cool to see people enjoying something you were a part of creating. I get to meet new people and hang out with my friends while at work.

Describe the general components of a hospitality marketing plan. What goes into promoting nightlife and restaurant experiences, and how does Native Sons Hospitality constantly build buzz and evolve to stay relevant?

To be honest with you, I stick to the old-school method of word of mouth. Of course we use social media as an advantage, but we like our community to be our mouthpiece. I know if we deliver a great experience, our supportive friends will help from there. I wouldn't have made it very far in this business if it wasn't for a strong, supportive group of friends and family.

Have there been measurable benefits from using social media? If so, what are they, and how have you measured them?

Social media is almost like people's report cards. The more followers, more likes, and more comments, the better you're perceived. I don't necessarily agree with it all the time, but it's definitely a necessary evil. I just like the idea you can connect directly with your guest.

What makes La Otra's nightlife experience different from a typical nightclub?

Nightclubs usually have some sort of pretentiousness from the minute you walk up. We wanted a space for everyone that enjoys a good time and music in an unconventional space.

What is different about Miami nightlife culture versus other party destinations, such as Las Vegas, Los Angeles, and New York City?

People in Miami like to have a good time. Anything goes.

Why did you decide to have La Otra provide a more personal and regulars-based vibe rather than VIPs and velvet ropes?

We didn't want to fool people with smoke and mirrors. We just want to show people a good time with good intentions.

What is your favorite memory from Sidebar [remodeled and renamed to La Otra]?

I have a bunch, but I think opening night was pretty special. I didn't think that many people would come out, and when they did, nothing felt better.

Who are some of your mentors, and why are they quality leaders in your eyes?

Roman Jones definitely taught me a lot about this business and life in general. He knows the importance of building a team. A best friend's father, Ernesto de la Fe, has always taken the time to listen to all my ideas and given me great guidance. My mom, dad, and stepdad are also strong mentors in my life.

Where do you see Native Sons Hospitality in the next five years?

I want to dive deeper into my current business and hopefully make them current places, long-lasting restaurants and bars. I'd like to also take a shot at a fast casual concept, one that I can potentially take to other markets.

CHAPTER 10:
MAIN TAKEAWAYS

In this final chapter, I will briefly sum up what stood out to me most from the interviews about the nightlife industry as a whole. I am thankful for the insight I gained through all these conversations and the overall opportunity to broaden my scope of knowledge about the nightlife business in a new, more dynamic format than school research papers. I also appreciate that some of the interviewees took the time to share personal stories and future plans off the record for my own enjoyment. Some of them have families and incredibly busy lives outside of running their venues at night, so I applaud them all for working day and night while also trying to live their own lives.

Throughout these ten interviews, we have learned about the experts' backgrounds, day-to-day routines, career challenges and accomplishments, and the impact they have made on the industry. To conclude this book, I wanted to note four major takeaways.

(1) Technological advances and social media need to be top priorities in the marketing plan.

(2) The behind-the-scenes operation, exterior of the brand, and quality of hospitality must evolve for every generation of partygoers.

(3) Passion and personality drive success in the nightlife industry.

(4) The business model needs to progress and get rid of outdated approaches.

Technology

Something extraordinary about nightlife is that it is one of the few experiences you cannot live through vicariously or obtain through the internet. You have to actually go out, be in the venue, connect with people, and hear the music live in order to have truly experienced it. This is why social media is a powerful nightlife marketing tool. Today's partygoers rely on social media to decide things like which restaurants to dine at, which clothes to buy, and where to party. However, the social media sphere is quite cluttered, so a venue's social media strategy and content can make or break someone's decision to go. The nightlife industry is inevitably going to change and adapt with society's rapidly advancing technology. The venues themselves will change stylistically and become more digitally infused, and the overall nightlife experience will certainly become more modernized as apps and novel platforms are developed to enhance partygoers' experiences. Partygoers back in the day did not even have cell phones to take pictures and videos in the club, but now people are glued to their phones, and it is a part of the nightlife experience. Nightclub operators and marketers need to acknowledge this because the photos and videos being posted are direct reflections of their nightlife brands.

Hospitality

The key to a successful nightlife venue is a precise mix of proper, behind-the-scenes business operations paired with a cool, photo-worthy aesthetic and quality music. Another thing that makes a venue truly stand out is its level of hospitality. Every partygoer should be treated like a VIP. I understand that exclusivity is a factor that contributes to a club's status, but too many bouncers and staff are mean-spirited to the point that people leave feeling disrespected and never want to return or recommend the club to anyone. These encounters are disappointing and can ruin a partygoer's night. Nightclub employees often mistake working in nightlife as a power trip, but the nightlife professionals who stay humble and treat everyone like a VIP succeed in the long run. I have come across too many cringe-worthy instances where I witness nightlife employees treating people harshly and unfairly. Any partygoer has the potential of being a big spender or of becoming a regular. For example, even if people are not dressed up in red-carpet attire or wearing a Rolex watch, they could potentially become regulars who party there every weekend and could bring groups of friends who spend money there and return every weekend too. Too many nightclubs do not think far enough ahead and do not realize that many of the so-called unimportant or low-paying young partygoers will eventually advance their careers, earn larger salaries, and spend their money at clubs where they are treated well. The clubs need to think long-term and always make good impressions. Customer loyalty is vital in this business, so it is a smart move for clubs to start partygoers young. The current and upcoming generations of partygoers are growing up with an overload of wellness trends and body consciousness due to the rise of social media, dating apps, and other platforms to which they continually expose themselves. The millennial and Gen Z generations still follow the "work hard, play hard" lifestyle, but some people choose to spend their play money on Barry's Bootcamp and seltzer rather than bottles of Dom Perignon. I wonder how the nightlife industry will adjust to these healthier and digitally literate populations.

Like I said in the marketing chapter, the partygoers help tell the nightclub's story, whether it is through word of mouth or word of eye. Therefore, everyone needs to enjoy themselves so they spread the positive review, and there is never a reason for them not to return. The music, crowd, and aesthetic can be great, but quality hospitality can make a place all that more memorable. You can keep a club fresh and relevant with a celebrity appearance or two, but the returning customers are the true VIPs.

Success

Another common thread from the interviews is that to be in this business, you need to love it. Due to the necessity to be at the venue often to ensure consistent and quality operation, the job becomes part of your lifestyle. In addition, if you want to break into this industry, you have to love nightlife and pay attention to the details of the experience the way the experts I spoke to do. You cannot take a back seat and trust that someone will throw the party the way you envision it. My Grandpa Saul always used to say, "If you want it done well, do it yourself."

Future

Overall, it is evident from this book that no two cities have the same nightlife culture, but they can all relate to some common themes. A night out at a nightclub is a complex production, similar to a Broadway show or concert tour. The future of nightlife needs to disrupt the norms, address the misconceptions, and increase inclusivity. I enjoy the current nightlife industry as it is, but I believe many aspects of it are outdated and unoriginal, and it has plenty of room to grow. It is a bit repetitive—the same DJs, bottle parades, overpriced drinks, dress code, clients, guest lists, staff, entertainment, and venue design. The business model needs to be more progressive, in my opinion. I truly believe that there is a plethora of opportunities for more diversity, inclusion, and general improvement that will open doors for venues to expand their clienteles and better their brands. At the end of the day, all partygoers want to feel comfortable going out, or else they will simply stay home and invite friends over. Current and upcoming generations will have different needs, and clubs need to adapt and attract them by offering an updated experience that they will think is worthy of spending money on. I hope these conversations have helped you in your current position or have inspired you as much as they have inspired me to contribute to the next era of nightlife. Cheers!

CPSIA information can be obtained
at www.ICGtesting.com
Printed in the USA
BVHW021138130321
602305BV00004B/76

9 781663 215642